951

A JOURNEY THROUGH ANCIENT CHINA

FROM THE NEOLITHIC
TO THE MING

HAN ZHONGMIN

HUBERT DELAHAYE

A JOURNEY THROUGH ANCIENT CHINA

DESIGNED BY

EMIL BÜHRER

MASSIMO GIACOMETTI

GALLERY BOOKS
An Imprint of W. H. Smith Publishers Inc.
112 Madison Avenue
New York City 10016

A Motovun Group Book

Originated and developed by:
Nebojsa-Bato Tomasevic

ISBN 0-8317-5225-4

Texts by: Han Zhongmin
            Hubert Delahaye
Designed by: Emil M. Bührer
              Massimo Giacometti
Photography: Miss Wang Lu,
   Chang Ping and others
Chief editor: Wang Fangzi
Co-production editor: Nevenka
Micunovic
Production manager: Lisa Clark
Printed and bound by:
Lito Terrazzi, Firenze, Italy
Photolithography by:
Scala, Istituto Fotografico Editoriale,
Firenze, Italy
Printed in Italy

TABLE OF CONTENTS

INTRODUCTION

BURIED TREASURES OF CHINA

MAJOR ARCHAEOLOGICAL FINDS

The most powerful force in Chinese archaeology is undoubtedly the mobilization of the minds of the people, particularly in the country. As K.C. Chang writes in his *Archaeology of Ancient China*: "When a communist regime is also nationalistic, in a country whose people are proud of their ancient heritage, conscious of history, and possessed of an antiquarian tradition, archaeology cannot help but boom. Many important sites have been found by farmers, who are known to be in the habit of promptly reporting the finds to the proper authorities..."

Major excavations undertaken in all parts of China from 1949 onwards, the year of the foundation of the People's Republic of China, have unearthed finds of tremendous significance, including the impressive underground mausoleum of the Emperor Qi Shi Huang Di.

From 1949 onwards, the year of the foundation of the People's Republic of China, major excavations have been carried out in every part of the country and archaeological teams have unearthed finds of major importance. The army of earthenware figures in the mausoleum of Qin Shi Huang has aroused the admiration of the whole world and is regarded as the eighth wonder, whilst objects such as the bronze lamp of the palace of Eternal Faithfulness and the flying horse are internationally famous. In this book, the principal discoveries of recent years are presented in chronological order of their age and are extensively illustrated in order to provide the reader with an overall view of the advances made by archaeological research in China. Some of the examples presented here are published for the first time.

Along with Egypt, Babylon and India, China, with its millennia of history and its extraordinary cultural heritage, is one of the most ancient of civilizations. The discoveries, often accidental, of the inheritance left by the ancestors of the Chinese people – relics which have often remained buried for centuries – have been of great assistance to historical research, supplementing it by closing gaps and supplying missing dates.

China has been inhabited since the dawn of time and Palaeolithic remains have been found in various provinces. That being said, the prelude to Chinese history is the Neolithic period. Up to now more than 6,000 Neolithic sites have been identified in various parts of the country and excavations have been undertaken at more than a hundred. The Neolithic culture was principally spread along the Huang Ho (Yellow River) and this was the cradle of a culture dating back five to six thousand years and known as the Yangshao culture. It takes its name from the village where it was discovered, in the district of Mianchi, in Henan, and the artefacts which characterize it are pieces of pottery painted with typical motifs. These everyday objects reveal the high degree of technical proficiency achieved by the Neolithic craftsmen. The changes and developments of form, decorative motifs and techniques of firing identify different cultures, enabling us to date them and revealing the relationships and reciprocal influences between the various groups. The remains unearthed in the excavations in the villages of Banpo and Jiangzhai, in the district of Lintong, Sha'anxi, are typical examples of the Yangshao culture. The Majiayao culture, discovered in the provinces of Gansu, Qinghai and others, is another culture of painted pottery and displays the influence of Yangshao.

In 1973 the remains of a primitive Neolithic culture dat-

Various pieces of Majiayao culture painted pottery have been discovered along the upper reaches of Yellow River in Gansu province.

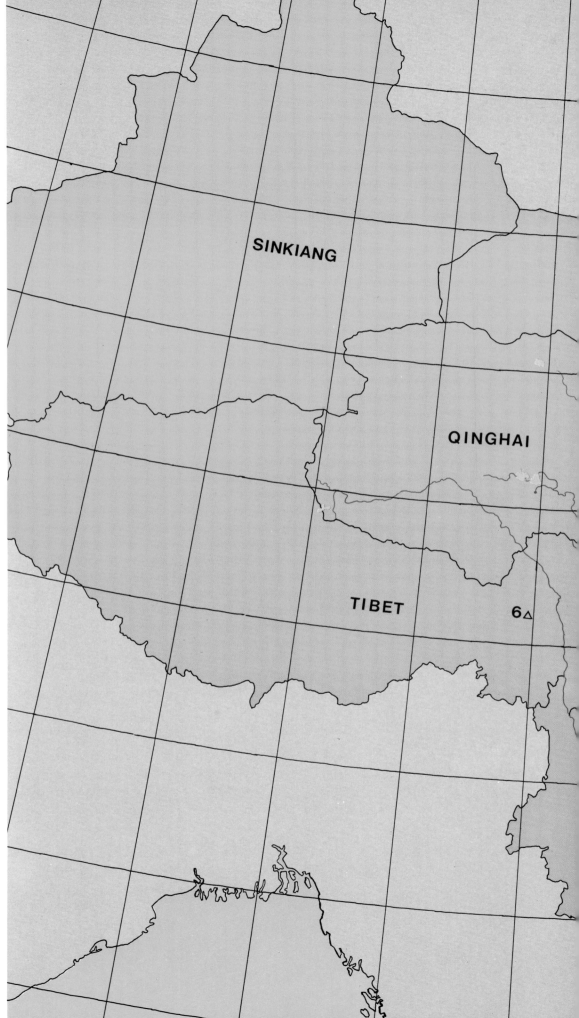

MAJOR ARCHAEOLOGICAL SITES

1. Banpo and Jiangzhai, Xi'an province
2. Yongdeng County, Gansu province
3. Liuwan, Qinghai province
4. Datong, Qinghai province
5. Hemudu, Zheiiang province
6. Kare, Tibet Autonomous Region
7. Yinxu, Henan province
8. Zhengzhou, Henan province
9. Zhouyuon, Sha'anxi province
10. Pingshan county, Hebei province
11. Changsha, Hunan province
12. Jinan, Hubei province
13. Lintong County, Sha'anxi province
14. Mancheng, Hebei province
15. Mawangdui, Hunan province
16. Shizhaishan, Yunnan province
17. Dabaotai, Beijing
18. Leitai, Gansu province
19. Xianyang, Sha'anxi province
20. Helinggel, Inner Mongolia
21. Xianggang, Guangdong province
22. Pingshao, Shanxi province
23. Sichuan province
24. Datong, Shanxi province
25. Cixian, Hebei province
26. Taiyuan, Shanxi province
27. Near Nanjing, Jiangsu province
28. Xi'an, Sha'anxi province
29. Xuanhua, Hebei province
30. Faku, Liaoning province
31. Suzhou, Jiangsu province
32. Jiaozhuo, Henan province
33. Beijing

1 — 6	△	Neolithic Period
7 — 9	●	Shang and Zhou Dynasties
10 — 12	○	Warring States Period
13	+	Qin Dynasty
14 — 23	■	Western Han and Eastern Han Dynasties
24 — 27	□	Northern and Southern Dynasties
28	▲	Tang Dynasty
29 — 33	▼	Modern times

Bronze horse's head discovered in 1980 to the west of the mausoleum of the First emperor.

The famous flying horse, a masterpiece of Han statuary.

ing from 4,000-5,000 BC were discovered in the village of Hemudu at Yuyao in Zhejiang. The specific characteristics of this culture were ceramics with incised motifs and the use of bones for divination. This important discovery demonstrated that, like the Yellow River, the Changjiang basin was also the home of an important primitive culture. Recently, Neolithic remains have been discovered at Kare in Tibet.

The Shang and Western Zhou dynasties span a period stretching from the sixteenth century to the eighth century BC. The work of excavating the ruins of Yin in the district of Anyang, Henan, which for almost three centuries was the capital of the Shang dynasty, was begun in 1928 and it has led to the discovery of numerous bones used for divination, which are the oldest examples of writing in China. Over the last three decades archaeological research has extended well beyond the ruins of Yin, building up a more balanced overall picture of Shang culture. In 1952 the remains of an ancient Shang city were discovered at Zengzhou, Henan. The bronze utensils displayed in this book are typical and show the high degree of skill that had been achieved in casting.

The Zhou tribe, originally from Chouyan, an area now in the modern districts of Qishan and Fufeng in Shanxi, supplanted the Shang. The Rong tribe conquered the capital of the Western Zhou in 771 BC and with the transfer of the capital to Loyi (modern Loyang, Henan), the Zhou tribe entered a new phase in its history, the Eastern Zhou. This marked the beginning of the Spring and Autumn and the Warring States eras (770-221 BC).

The wars which followed in the district of Zhouyan destroyed the city completely but bronze objects from the Han dynasty have been found in the area adjacent to it. In recent years the area has been investigated and systematically excavated, leading to the discovery of, amongst other features, the foundations of a temple of the ancestors and a great palace of the Western Zhou. Archaeologists consider the archaic bronzes of the Shang and Zhou to be symbols of religious authority and power. These bronzes are divided into four categories: musical instruments, weapons, utensils and ornaments for horses and carriages.

In the Spring and Autumn and the Warring States eras Chinese society underwent profound transformations. After the transfer of the Zhou to Loyi, the Qin state in the west rapidly increased in power with the annexation of the Rong tribe and various vassal states. To the south, the Chu state occupied a vast area of territory. To the north the Jin state absorbed more than 30 vassal states and then, in its turn, split into the three states of Han, Zhao and Wei. To the east was the state of Qi and to the north-east that of Yan. It was a period of continuous warfare during which the various lords fought for power and struggled to achieve hegemony.

Recently their sites have begun to be studied and excavated intensely. In the present book we will be presenting finds from the tomb of a prince of Zongshan, excavated at Pingshan, Hebei and from the tomb of the Marquis of Zeng at Sinxian, Hubei, which dates from the beginning of the Warring States era. Furthermore, it is worth recalling the archaeological discoveries of Jinan, capital of the Chu state, in the district of Jangling, Hubei. The numerous tombs in the area around the city have provided investigators with important information on Chu culture and various lacquers are included here — lacquer being an art form that was highly developed and flourishing at this time, whereas ceramics and bronzes were less prominent.

In 221 BC Qin Shi Huang, the First Emperor of the Qin dynasty, succeeded in ending the divisions of the preceding period and created the first unified and centralized feudal state in Chinese history. On the basis of historical documents, work on the imperial mausoleum on Mount Li began the moment Shi ascended the throne and continued for 38 years. In 210 BC, the year of his death, it was still not complete. In 1974 a vast multitude of terracotta statues was

Terracotta warrior dating from the Northern and Southern Dynasties period.

Quilin, the Chinese unicorn, standing in front of the tomb of the Chen Emperor at Ganjiaxiang, Nanjing.

A guan vessel, *a typical example of Tang three-coloured pottery, with a lid in the form of a pagoda.*

discovered in three pits about a mile from the mausoleum. They comprised more than 7,000 life-size soldiers and horses, arranged in order of battle, and forming a magnificent underground military museum. We also include here two bronze teams of horses, chariots and charioteers, recently discovered on the west side of the museum.

In the last 30 years excavations have brought to light a large number of Han tombs all over China. The most significant are those of Lingshan at Mancheng, Hebei and that of Mawangdui near Changsha, Hunan, which both date from the Western Han dynasty. The wealth of objects found in them bear witness to the complexity of funerary practices at this time. In addition to a selection of the more interesting artefacts (jade funerary garments, funerary standards, military maps painted on silk, etc.) there are also illustrations of bronzes and other finds from Shihjiashan, Jiuning district, Yunnan, which reflect the material culture of ethnic minorities — it is the first time that such objects have been found in Han tombs. The tomb of the king of the Southern Yue is also worth noting (modern Xianggang in the city of Guangzhou). Recently excavated, it was found to contain about 2,000 jade vessels and more than 500 bronzes, making it one of the most important tombs in the region.

With the collapse of Han power, feudal society went through a further phase of development, marked by rivalry between different states. At first China was split into Three Kingdoms, then the Western Jin dynasty was established. This was short-lived. In northern China the Toba tribe established the Northern Wei dynasty (386-534), which was to be followed by the Eastern Wei (534-557), the Northern Qi (550-557) and the Northern Zhou (557-581); collectively known as the Northern Dynasties. Under the Six Dynasties, which dominated the southern part of the country from 220 to 589, the middle and lower sections of the Yangzi developed economically. Examples of painted lacquers, terracotta figurines, sculptures, incised bricks and celadon ware illustrate the art of this period.

The period of the Sui and Tang dynasties (581-907) marked an unprecedented flowering of Chinese culture. In the seventh century, the capital cities of Chang'an and Loyang were the most prosperous and cosmopolitan cities of their time. The three-coloured porcelains with their brilliant tints obtained by oxidation at low temperature are the typical products of this period.

From the tenth century to the thirteenth century a vast part of northern China was dominated by the kingdoms of Liao and Jin, who were in conflict with the Nothern and Southern Song dynasties. Items unearthed from a Liao tomb in the district of Faku, Liaoning and in the district of Xuanhua, Hebei, included various artefacts and ornaments; whereas splendid porcelains and Buddhist artefacts have been found beneath the Song pagodas of the district Dingxian, Hebei and at Shuzhou, Jiangsu.

The artistic production of the Yuan is documented by a series of vividly realistic carved tomb bricks. Thirteen of the sixteen emperors of the Ming dynasty (1368-1644) are buried in the splendid imperial mausoleum which is sited in a valley on the outskirts of Peking. The tomb of the Emperor Wan Li was excavated in 1956-8 and it is now open to the public, who may admire its jades, porcelains, gold and silver artefacts, as well as fine silks. The book ends with illustrations of the most precious objects of the last Chinese dynasty. The systematic work carried out over the last 35 years in settlements and tombs in various parts of the country has brought enormous quantities of material to light. The discoveries illustrated in this volume are the major ones of recent years and are intended to offer the reader an overall impression of the historical development of Chinese art.

On the following page: The East Lake of Shaoxing in the province of Zheijang, which was used for centuries as a stone quarry. The Neolithic site of Hemudu was discovered in this province.

Ming vase with blue and white decoration and a lid with a double dragon intertwined with lotus branches. Fine clay and a brilliant glaze.

THE YELLOW RIVER A CRADLE OF CHINA

NEOLITHIC PERIOD

The Yellow River basin seems to have been the centre of gravity of the lands of China since remote antiquity. The history of this river and that of China display surprising parallels. Rich in alluvium, the promise of fertility, its floods could nevertheless devastate the country more surely than a band of invaders.

Various Yangshao culture sites, in particular Banpo and Jiangzhai, have yielded numerous pottery fragments with markings incised either before or after firing.

Archaeological research on the Neolithic settlements has provided important information on the early stages of the history of China. Up to the present moment, more than 6,000 Neolithic sites have been discovered and excavations have been carried out at more than a hundred. The study of the geographical distribution of the settlements and their stratification, and the various types of material excavated have enabled archaeologists to determine the nature, age, origin and development of various remains and their inter-relationships, and to trace, on a scientific basis, the historical development of the beginnings of Chinese civilization.

The valley of the Huang-ho is the cradle of China. The Neolithic finds discovered recently in Cishan, Wúan district, Hebei and at Peiligang, Xinzheng district, Henan are some 7,000-8,000 years old on the basis of C14 dating and have led to the proposal of a "Cishan-Peiligang culture". The foundation of houses, pits for provisions, kilns, cemeteries, shovels, scythes, mills, seeds, as well as the skeletons of pigs and dogs which have been discovered in dozens of localities, demonstrate that at this period there was a primitive agriculture, the breeding of domestic animals and a relatively settled way of life. The discovery of this culture has allowed archaeology to fill gaps between the end of the Palaeolithic and the middle of the Neolithic.

The term Yangshao culture covers the Neolithic remains which are principally found along the upper and middle Huang-ho. One of the characteristic features of the Yangshao culture is the production of pottery painted with a variety of elegant motifs. The culture takes its name from the village in the district of Mianchi, in Henan province, in which it was discovered. It was very widespread and displayed numerous differences in the course of its long development but it is usual to divide it into two main types. These are the Banpo type at the beginning and the Miadigou type in the middle, although the two often occur together at particular sites. The excavations carried out in the villages of Banpo and Jiangzhai, on the edge of modern Xǐan, in the course of five seasons from 1954 to 1957, have covered an area of 10,000 square metres and have unearthed the remains of more than 200 pits, 46 houses, 6 kilns, 250 tombs, 7,900 tools and 1,000 utensils in a good state of preservation and capable of being restored. For the most part, the utensils are of stone or bone and include axes, hoes, ploughs, arrow heads, fishing nets and hooks, knives for harvesting and cutting. The vessels for everyday use, whose variety matches the diversity of requirements, are mostly pottery and may be divided into three categories on the basis of the material used, a coarse, sandy pottery, a fine, clay pottery and a fine, hard, sandy pottery.

The painted pottery of Banpo has a simplicity and vivacity that is still apparent and it conjures up the lives of the craftsmen who made it: so the chequer patterns reflect fish nets or the scales of fish or weaving, waves or mountains on the horizon appear in the sinuous lines and deer which

Ping *vessel in painted terracotta (height 24.5 cm.), modelled on a gourd and decorated with fish and birds.*

gallop, fish and frogs ready to leap evoke the nervous humour of the hunter.

The more recent Longshan culture was discovered in the city of the same name in the district of Licheng, Shandong province. It developed along the middle and lower stretches of the Yellow River in about 2,000 BC and its remains indicate a marked advance in the techniques of pottery making. The use of the wheel allowed the production of black, thin-walled pottery. Found over a wide area of distribution, the Longshan culture displays marked regional characteristics. In the provinces of Henan, Sha'anxi and Shanxi there are derivations from the Yangshao culture, whereas in Shandong and other coastal areas it is thought to be a development of the eastern Dawenkou culture, closely linked to the Qingliangang culture of the Yangtze and Huaihe valleys.

The Dawenkou culture was discovered in 1959 south of Tai'an in Shandong province. It dates from between 4,000 and 2,000 BC and occurred in Shandong and the northern parts of the provinces of Jiangsu and Anhui. The objects discovered in Shandong are from a late Dawenkou culture and represent a transition towards the Longshan culture. The painted motifs on the pottery are thought by some to be the earliest examples of writing found in China, whilst others regard them as the totemic symbols of particular clans.

A very ancient culture, dating from 4,000-5,000 BC, has been discovered at Hemudu, Yuyao district in Zhejiang, and it provides evidence that the lower Changjiang valley had an advanced culture and was another of the cradles of Chinese civilization. Excavations have unearthed large numbers of agricultural tools made of animal bones — relics of extensive farming and water regulation. Dwellings built on piles indicate a settled way of life and a thick paddy layer with rice stems and leaves shows that this cereal was already being farmed. The Hemudu culture subsequently developed into the Majiabang and Liangzhu cultures.

The settlements of the Daxi and Qujialing culture disco-

Numerous animal figurines have been found at Hemudu, including this pig (length 4-9 cm.), a motif which is also incised on everyday utensils.

Terracotta spinning wheels, most are decorated.

vered along the middle section of the Changjiang partially overlap with those of the Yangshao and Longshan cultures and were closely linked. In particular, the painted motifs of Daxi pottery show the influence of Yangshao. The Qujialing culture is known for its thin-walled painted pottery which has much in common with Longshan pottery in its shapes.

In southern China the remains of the following cultures have been found: Shanbei in Jiangxi, Shixia in Guangdong and Tanshishan in Fujian. A common feature of all of them is a type of red pottery with decorative elements pressed in with cord, employing relatively primitive techniques and fired at low temperatures. These peoples lived by hunting, fishing and gathering – no signs of agricultural production have been found. The tropical and subtropical environment kept the economic and cultural development of the region behind that of the Huanghe and Changjiang valleys. In the final phase pottery with impressed geometric motifs was being produced whilst the central plains were beginning the Shang and Zhou periods.

In the northern part of China, from the north-east to Xingjiang, the grassy plateaux were suitable for grazing by livestock and it is in this area that numerous microlithic finds – typical of a nomadic economy – have been made. These include the Hongsham culture and the Fuhe culture along the Lahoe river. In Tibet, at Kare, south-east of Chengdu, foundations of houses, pottery, jade and bone objects have been found, which, in their characteristics and style show a similarity to the Neolithic finds of the Yellow River and the Yangzi.

The complex pattern of interactions and influences between various types of Neolithic culture finally results in a trend towards cultural uniformity. As a whole, these cultures form a magnificent group and they were to form the basis of the development of the splendid, unified civilization of Ancient China.

Terracotta jar with a human figure in relief (height 33.4 cm., diameter 19 cm.), decorated with large rings and a reticulated motif.

The Painted Pottery
of the Yangshao Culture

All the objects illustrated here are from the excavations in the villages of Banpo (below) and Jiangzhai, on the edge of Xi'an, Sha'anxi province.

Right: Guan *terracotta jar with pointed bottom and flowing, sinuous geometric decorations (9.4 cm. diameter, height 21.3 cm.).*
Below: *Terracotta bowl decorated with fish and frog motifs (34.5 cm. diameter).*

Opposite, left: *Painted terracotta* ping *water vessel in the form of a gourd (24.5 cm. height).*

Right: *Thin-walled* bo *basin with a straight mouth — narrower than of* pen *bowls. The upper part of the outer surface is decorated with geometric motifs (diameter 14.5 cm., height 9 cm.)*

22

The site of Banpo, which was discovered in 1952, gives an excellent idea of the state of civilization achieved in the basins of the Yellow River below the Ordos loop and its tributary, the Wei, during the Neolithic period and doubtless before. Although the site of Banpo, which flourished between 5,000 and 3,000 BC, may be assigned to what is known as

the Yangshao culture (for historical reasons: it was at Yangshao-cun, further east, that the first sherds of the characteristic "red pottery" were discovered in 1920), it is Banpo which provides the fullest picture and the greatest amount of information concerning the surroundings and the way of life of the ancestors of the Chinese. The two hundred or so houses and granaries of "halfway village" were half underground and varied in shape, being pyramidal, square or round, and about five metres in diameter. Some had an entrance passage and one might ask oneself whether, as with the passage of burial chambers which appeared later, this was linked to the position of the occupant. All the houses had an oven for cooking food, as did a long communal house situated in the centre of the village and whose function is unclear. Six pottery kilns were built to the east of the village, near the deep ditch which surrounded the group of dwellings. The total area of Banpo is calculated at about five hectares.

23

Objects Used in Everyday Life: Functional Forms and Aesthetic Experimentation

Two guan *jars, the upper one has a pattern of angled triangles, the lower one has incised decoration.*

Centre: *Pottery bowl painted with a net motif and the mask of a human figure surmounted by an ornament and flanked by two fish (diameter 44.5 cm., height 17 cm.).*

Below: *Water vessel with a narrow mouth and a pointed base (height 43 cm.); incised decoration.*

Opposite: *This* hu *vase is outstanding for the purity of its line, the care of its finishing, its smooth surface and its narrow mouth in the form of a mushroom.*

THE LOWER YANGZI

The technique of land clearance and soil fertilization of the people of Banpo often consisted of slash and burn. This method of land use is still employed in Malaysia (*ladang*) and Vietnam (*ray*) and it exhausts the soil very quickly so that one would imagine that crops would have to be frequently rotated, obliging the cultivators to be somewhat mobile.

It was in this area, amongst others, that the Neolithic cultures of the maritime provinces of Shandong and Zhejiang, known as the Longshan culture, made decisive technological advances. These cultures appear more recent than those of Yangshao and in fact C14 dating places them only in the third millennium. They developed their technology extensively, making more sophisticated tools, better fishhooks, finer pottery, thanks to the adoption of the wheel.

Polygonal fu *brazier (height 22.8 cm.) intended for cooking food, found with traces of burnt wood at the bottom.*

Oval bone cup with an incised interlaced motif, silk worm and two symmetrical openings near the rim.

Their firing techniques also made great progress, so much so that the "black pottery" typical of the Longshan cultures attained a plastic quality without equal for its period. Over the centuries the pottery became the work of professionals who worked for artistic as well as utilitarian ends. For example, they produced pottery for the collective religious ceremonies which were more than just festivities associated with sowing and harvesting and already seem to be linked with the cult of the ancestors. Religious magical cults began to appear, with prophecies engraved on charmed animal bones and subsequently during the Shang Dynasty, on turtle shells. Villages were by now fortified by walls and palissades, and social classes became clearer, above all identifiable by their particular mode of burial (coffin or double interment) and their funerary jades.

All this social organization and technology gradually lifted the ancestors of the Chinese out of the primitive world. It is certain that the local cultures of the middle and lower Yellow River played a pioneering role in this slow evolution. Because of the absence of geographical barriers one cannot doubt their influence on the southern Neolithic cultures such as those of Hemudu and then those of Qinliangang, Lianghzu and all the others which occupied the provinces of Jiangsu, Zhejiang and as far as the coasts of Taiwan. However, this influence is difficult to discern because these middle and lower Yangzi cultures were both ancient and original in their features. In particular they had the benefit of a dense and relatively stable hydrographic network thanks to some large lakes (since the Yellow River often flooded catastrophically and deviated hundreds of kilometres from its course). This stability obviously played a part in the early growth of rice culture and – with the help of the climate – of such tropical crops as melons and peanuts. The people of the Yangzi delta possessed large numbers of water buffaloes and were well versed in fishing, as is apparent from the array of fish-hooks, harpoons and nets that has been found.

Numerous animal figurines have been found at Hemudu, including sheep, fish, swallows, dogs and swine.

Below: The same images are found incised on both sides of the square bo bowl (height 11.7 cm.).

Bone whistles (length, 6-10 cm.), with from one to five holes, these were both musical instruments and used to call animals.

29

THE BORDERS AND THE STEPPE

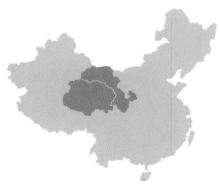

The spread of the Yangshao and Longshan cultures towards the steppes and above all to the borders of Central Asia – particularly eastern Gansu – appears clearer. Here again, it is pottery which provides the main evidence. The red and black spiral, rose, lozenge and ware motifs of the friezes on pottery utensils discovered in sites such as those of Majiayao or Banshan achieve great formal beauty in their stylization which often exceeds that of the pottery of the Central Plain. Such features, however, are deceptive. These round and swollen jars, these rather stereotyped vases are far from being as elegant as the "black pottery" of Shandong discussed earlier. Functional above all else, these utensils reflect the less refined life of the peasants and herdsmen of the borders of Central Asia and the steppes.

But the relative distance of these zones from the Central Plain did not visibly pose problems. Gansu, one should not

forget, was the starting and finishing point of what was to become the Silk Route and the contacts with western Asia certainly pre-date the opening up of this route. Chinese scholars, to whom a sinocentric outlook is often second nature, very rarely mention the striking similarities between the decorative motifs of pottery found in Lanzhou, Jiuquan and in other sites in Gansu and those of the pottery traditionally made in sites near the Caspian Sea. Likewise, one cannot help but note the similarities between the motifs and forms of the Neolithic pottery unearthed in the northern zones of Inner Mongolia and Manchuria and those of the Siberian cultures. One final example, which bears directly on the Bronze Age, somewhat moderates the theories fondly advanced by Chinese scholars, according to which the closed cultures of the Central Plain alone gave rise to Chinese civilization. This example is a granary at Wuwei in Gansu, in which, a dozen or so years ago, some knives, chisels and awls were discovered made of an almost pure copper. These were amongst the earliest metal objects discovered in China (dated at around 2000 BC).

Above: Jar with a relief of a human figure. Decorated in its upper part with large circles filled with a reticulate pattern; discovered in the excavations at Liuwan in 1974 (height 33.4 cm., diameter 19 cm.).
Right: Terracotta jar with interlaced decorative motifs discovered in 1975 at Jiawan in the district of Ledu, province of Qinghai (diameter 15 cm., height 20 cm.).

Opposite, left: Painted terracotta basin with dancers holding hands and arranged in three horizontal lines. Excavated in 1973 at Datong, Qinghai province, it is one of the best depictions of human activity.
Right: Pottery vessel with an elongated neck and a single handle. Brought to light in 1976 in the course of the excavations at Liuwan, Qinghai province (diameter 7.7 cm., height 19 cm.).

The large number of pottery items found along the upper stretches of the Yellow River in the province of Gansu are from what is known as the "Yangshao of Gansu" culture or the Majiayao culture. Typical pieces are the large rounded water vessels decorated with strong geometric, reticulated or spiral motifs, with broad mouths and one or two handles.

Top right: *The painted jar is un-usual in having a constriction in the middle and is decorated with a motif of parallel lines, grids and circles.*

Right: *This painted pottery cup has a stylized human face on the handle (diameter 12.3 cm., height 24.6 cm.). It was found in 1973 in the district of Vongdeng, Gansu province.*

Above: *A coloured piece of pottery with red and black geometric patterns of the Macheng type.*

Opposite: *A tripod jar of red pottery, used as a cooking utensil in the late Neolithic.*

TIBET

At the village of Kare, near the town of Chamdo in eastern Tibet, is the site of a Neolithic settlement dating from 4,600 years ago. In an area of about two acres large quantities of stone implements and earthenware and bone utensils have been found, as well as the bones of oxen and sheep. In several cases the design of the earthenware pots is very similar to the design of those dating from the same period found in the Yellow River valley.

Right: *Double vase in the form of an animal, unearthed at the Neolithic site of Kare.*

Opposite, top: *Grindstone.*
Below: *foundation of Neolithic dwelling.*

Following page: *View of the peaks which dominate the roof of the world.*

THE MASTERS OF BRONZE CASTING

SHANG AND ZHOU DYNASTIES

Detail of a gong vessel: lid in the form of a giraffe's head, with a small dragon between the horns and phoenixes to the sides.

The Xia dynasty, according to written sources, existed between the twenty-first century and the sixteenth century BC and over the four or more centuries that it held sway it had 17 kings between Yu the Great and Jie, however, despite much recent research, no direct proof of its existence has emerged.

On the other hand a culture, the Erlitou in Yanshi, has been discovered which matches the mythical dynasty both geographically and in time. A deep layer, indicating a settled population living at the site for a considerable period of time, was found and contained stone artefacts in the main, although there were also the remains from castings, moulds and fragments of pottery. Similarly, small bronze objects such as swords, bells, arrow heads and hooks have also been excavated. Extremely primitive, they display little variety and lack both decoration and inscriptions. Small and thin, they are usually modelled on artefacts of the same type made of pottery, stone, bone, shells, etc. This period therefore marks the beginning of the Bronze Age.

In the station of Wangchenggang, in the district of Dengfeng, Henan province, at the southern end of the mountains of Shongshan, the existence of a castle has been discovered which some experts believe may be a remnant of a Xia building. In recent years, it has provided further clues for research. A fragment of a bronze vessel discovered here is thought to be the oldest ever found on the central plains, but its form is difficult to identify.

According to legend, the Shang tribe was contemporary with the Xia but lived in a different area. The first historical Chinese dynasty, which spanned the period from the sixteenth century to the eleventh century BC, was founded after the Xia had been overcome. The ruins of Yin, northwest of the present city of Anyang, Henan province, was the capital of the late Shang dynasty for 273 years. The excavations were begun in 1928 and since then 15 seasons of digs have been carried out. From the foundation of the People's Republic, large-scale excavations carried out on a scientific basis have demonstrated that this station not only had Shang layers but also the remains of a preceding period.

On the southern bank of the river Huanshui, near the village of Xiaotun, the complex of palaces and temples of the ancestors of the Shang has been found, together with various workshops and pits for provisions, as well as large numbers of turtle shells and animal bones used in divinations. The best preserved of the tombs that have been investigated over the last fifty years is the tomb of a member of the Shang royal family excavated in the village of Xiaotun in 1976. It has yielded the largest number of artefacts, particularly exquisitely made bronzes and jades. On the north bank, near the villages of Houjia and Wuguan, is

Jia *tripod (91 cm. high), with uprights in the form of phoenixes; it was used as a vessel for containing and also warming wine.*

the burial ground of the royal family and the nobility. To the east of the royal necropolis there is an area specially reserved for sacrifices to the ancestors — excavations have revealed that 1,178 slaves were buried alive in 191 pits over an area of 4,700 square metres.

The remains of the walls of a city from the early Shang

The ruins of Yinxu, the capital of the late Shang dynasty, stretch along both banks of the river Hanghui. The remains of the first Shang dynasty have also been discovered at Zhengzou, in the province of Henan. This is probably the oldest city to have been found in China.

period have been found at Zhengzhou in Henan. The walls were made of layers of compressed earth, had a circumference of almost seven km. (just under 5 miles) and varied in height between 1 and 9 metres (3 to 27 ft.). The remains of buildings and a large tumulus of compressed earth are to be found in the north-east part of the city, and outside the city workshops for bronze casting and polishing bones have been discovered. This is one of the oldest known cities in China but other cities with similar cultural features have been found at Pauloncheng, Huangpi district, Hubei province and at Wucheng, Qinjiang, Jiangxi and it has become clear that the Shang culture, which was once believed to be restricted to the middle region of the Huanghe, in fact extended through large parts of the valley of the Chanjiang and of the Hansui, where it persisted for a long time.

The Shang tombs discovered in the region of Peking and

in the provinces of Shandong and Hebei have provided new insights into Shang culture. In the village of Taixi, Gaodeng district, Hebei province, a bronze *yue* axe has been discovered with an iron edge. The iron has turned out to be meteoric in origin and to have been forged and fixed to the bronze by a casting process. This provides proof that at

that time the characteristics of iron were already known and it was possible to forge and fix it to a bronze object by casting. A similar artefact has been found in a Shang tomb at Liujiahe, Pinggu district, Beijing.

In the Shang period the art of bronze reached its mature phase with a sophisticated technology. The objects display a great variety of original and refined forms with splendid decorations. In the ruins of Yin a ritual cauldron 133 cm. high and weighing 875 kg. has been found. This is the largest bronze object ever unearthed in China. The technique of glazed pottery also reached its peak with the emergence of proto-porcelain. At Zhengzhou a *zun* wine vessel with a blue glaze has been unearthed — it is an example of proto-porcelain which is 3,500 years old. Engraving on jade is another technique which reached a high degree of perfection.

The Zhou tribe, originally from the loess plateaux between the Jingshui and Weishui rivers, was forced to move into Sha'anxi under the pressure of northern tribes of the Rong and the Di. Once established in Zhouyuan, a highly fertile area well suited to agriculture between the modern districts of Qishan and Fufeng, they began to expand east, subsequently establishing their capital at Feng and then at Hao on the river Fengshui. In about 1027 BC King Wu led a punitive expedition against the Shang kingdom to the east and, after the decisive battle of Muye, which marked the end of the Shang, the Zhou established an eastern capital at Loyi, in order to reinforce their authority over the conquered territories. With the expansion of its influence, the Zhou state become much more powerful than the Shang.

Prior to 1949 virtually no archaeological research had been done on the Western Zhou. The research and excavations carried out on both banks of the river Fengshui began in 1951. They were followed in 1953 by research into the remains of the Shang capital along the river Jianhe in the suburbs of modern Loyang. More recently, remains of Zhou palaces and temples of the ancestors have been unearthed in the station of Zhouyuan, where a large quantity of

The archaeological discoveries of recent years have shown the historical reality of the Shang dynasty, who were regarded as legendary only a few decades ago.

oracular bones and bronzes have also been found.

Zhouyaun is situated on the southern spurs of Mount Qishan and is washed to the south by the river Weihe. It extends for about three km. from east to west and about five km. from north to south. Over the last three decades numerous archaeological investigations have been carried out on this site and large-scale digging began in February 1976.

The discovery of oracle bones and the foundations of a temple of the ancestors in the area around the modern village of Fengchu has confirmed the site of the capital of the first Western Zhou dynasty, Qiyi. In the vicinity of the village of Yuntang, Fufeng district, workshops for the carving of bone, the casting of copper and pottery, as well as the remains of the dwellings of the common people have been found. Densely scattered tombs and pits for chariots are also found in the village Hejia, in the district of Qishan. Qiyi lost its position as the capital when King Wen moved to Feng, however, since it was the birthplace of the dynasty and the seat of the temple of the acestors, many of the ancestors were buried there. In the final phase of the Western Zhou, in the face of the Rong invasion, the dynasty moved east, and Qiyi was reduced to ruins. Over the years, the bronzes which have been discovered here have mostly been found in the ruins of dwellings in the surrounding area, where they may have been hidden by nobles when fleeing from the disasters of war.

In their bronzes the Zhou inherited the Shang tradition, whilst adding new forms and decorative motifs. The forms include *gui* vessels with square bases, halberds, swords and bells. The decoration is dominated by the *taotie* mask, with a variety of motifs. The bronzes often bear long inscriptions which give the history of the occasion for which they were cast, whether for the owners and their family, for sacrificial purposes, on the occasion of the departure on an expedition or as payment. These inscriptions, which are markedly longer than late Shang ones, provide valuable

He vessel *(height 29 cm.) with an inscription on the lid relating to a sale of land during the reign of King Gong of the Zhou dynasty.*

historical information. Highly important bronzes, with a considerable amount of historical detail concerning the Western Zhou dynasty, can be read on the mass of bronzes excavated near the village of Dongjia, in the district of Qishan. They include the *Weihe* pot and the *Wei Ding* tripod, which bear inscriptions relating to earthly transactions; a *yi* ewer records a trial and a court verdict. A group of bronzes belonging to the Wei family have been unearthed in the village of Zhuanghai, Fufeng district. The *pan* bowl made by Quiang records events relating to the first kings of the Western Zhou dynasty and the history of the Wei family. In the middle period of the Western Zhou wine vessels gradually disappear and the decorative schemes are reworked — the images of animals show a tendency towards realism whilst the tiny, complex motifs are reduced. By the end of the period the bronzes were tending to become simpler and more practical whilst animal motifs became increasingly abstract. The bronzes of the middle and late periods display a similarity of form, decoration and composition of the inscriptions and occur together in groups or series — an indication that the ritual practices and rules of the aristocracy underwent a marked change with respect to those of the first period. Important Zhou tombs with numerous bronze objects and other artefacts have also been found in other places, such as Liulihe near Beijing, on the hill of Yandun in the district of Dantu, Jiangsu province; in the district of Lingyuan, province of Liaoning; the city of Tunxi, Anhui and in the district of Lingtai, Gansu.

In the early Zhou period the bronze technology was rather poor. King Wu, after having defeated the Shang kindgom, seized many of its bronzes and those of its vassal states. To begin with, Zhou bronzes remain very much in the traditional Shang styles and it is only later that they begin to diverge. The Zhou dynasty far exceeded the Shang in the numbers of bronzes made and the numbers of workshops. Whereas Shang bronzes had elaborate decorative motifs and thick walls, Zhou ones tended towards simple

Detail of a bronze bird's head with a decorative motif of scales.

48

decoration and thin walls, emphasizing functional requirements. As has already been mentioned there was also a difference in the length of the inscriptions. The majority of late Shang inscriptions comprised between one and five or six words and the longest did not exceed fifty, whereas long and highly informative inscriptions were common on Western Zhou bronzes. A *ding* cooking vessel from the reign of King Kang, for example, bears an inscription of 291 words and the Mao Gong *ding* from the reign of King Xuan has one of 497 words. So far as other artefacts are concerned, the range of wine vessels decreases whilst the first examples of the *zhong* bell, the large *bo* bell, the *fu* food plate, the *xu* food plate, halberds, swords and scythes begin to appear.

Glazed Zhou pottery marks a clear advance over the Shang work whose qualities it inherited. It approached porcelain in being fired at high temperatures and is characterized by its high density and low porosity.

The lacquers and jades also represent a step forward over those of the Shang. Elegant jade objects were highly valued and used by the nobility not only as ornaments but also as ritual vessels.

With the transfer east of the capital, the dynasty assumed the title of the Eastern Zhou and lost control of several duchies. At the same time a period of great turbulence and profound change began. This is known as the Spring and Autumn era and was followed by the Warring States period.

Above and left: Two recurrent decorative motifs, which are drawn with varying degrees of abstraction, in primitive Chinese bronzes: they are respectively the phoenix and the wolverine, the taotie.

SHANG DYNASTY

18TH-12TH CENTURY B.C.

It is common today, when there is abundant archaeological evidence of its existence, to refer to the Shang dynasty as the first of the pre-imperial Chinese dynasties. However, although there is no conclusive evidence to associate one of the late Neolithic cultures of the Central Plain, particularly the Erlitou, with the Xia dynasty, which traditionally preceded the Shang, it should not be assumed that the Xia are purely mythical. After all, many orientalists were sceptical about the Shang before the old legends were confirmed by the excavations in the 20s at Anyang, the last capital of the Shang, established soon after 1400 BC.

Throughout almost the entire length of its sovereignty the clan of the Shang controlled the province of Henan, largely populated by the peoples of the Yi tribes, and its immediate surroundings, or in other words a large part of the lower Yellow River basin. What, at the outset, was simply a local chieftainry succeeded in subjecting for almost 450 years the other peoples of the Central Plain as well as the "barbarian" tribes – proto-Turks, proto-Tibetans, proto-Tunguse – belonging to markedly different ethnic groups.

Leaving factual history to one side – some of the details of which are uncertain – there are two important questions to be answered, namely: how were the Shang able to establish their supremacy so suddenly and for such a long period, and what were their principal contributions to Chinese culture? The development of bronze working may provide part of the answer to both these questions. As has been said, the techniques associated with the casting and, in particular, the alloying of metals could have been introduced rather than have originated in the lower Yellow River basin. However, it was in this region, which already had a certain technological lead, that some clans, seeing the military advantage it could bring them, were able to develop the industry. The oldest bronzes that have come to light are weapons: arrows, parts of a chariot and, above all, halberds, the dominant weapon in battle at this period. Powerful chiefs rapidly formed a city-dwelling warrior and hunting aristocracy much more advanced than their rural neighbours, where agricultural implements long continued to be made from stone. Urban architecture made considerable progress but so too did the applied sciences such as the calendar; the special treatment reserved for the new elite during rites, ceremonies and funerals; was not without effect on the development of a bronze industry. The customers for these bronzes were tremendous huntsmen and it was not uncommon for 300 or 400 animals (deer, wild boar, bears, tigers) to be slain in a single day. This activity was naturally reflected in the bronze objects, which took on zoomorphic forms which were as varied as the natural bestiary.

Bronze craftsmen began to sign their masterpieces with a graphic sign or an emblem, and dedications also began to appear. The dedications were in general fairly short until the end of the Shang — a few words along the lines of: "To my principal mother Wu", or "To my father Gui", "To my grandfather Gao". These last two dedications were more frequent and they testify to the developments taking place in the ideas of filial piety and also the cult of the ancestors. These bronzes rapidly ceased to be purely utilitarian and became, because of their temporal and spiritual power, a part of an extensive funerary, ritual and sacrificial world. Although the religious beliefs of this period were fairly imprecise, the funeral rites of the noble classes took on a sumptuousness which prefigured the extravagances of the tomb of the First Emperor some 12 or 13 centuries later. There are numerous, richly decorated burial chambers where bronzes, human and animal sacrifices, silks, jade (still imported from Central Asia) and valuable objects abounded and greeted the tomb robbers who have so often beaten archaeologists to the funeral sites of the Shang.

One day perhaps the following passage from the historical chronicle Zuozhuan, from the third year of Xuangong, will be borne out by new archaeological discoveries: "Anciently, when Xia was distinguished for its virtue, the distant regions sent pictures of the [remarkable] objects in them. The nine pastors sent in the metal of their provinces and the tripods were cast, with representations on them of those objects. All the objects were represented, and [instructions were given] of the preparations to be made in reference to them, so that the people might know the sprites and evil things. Thus the people, when they went among the rivers, marshes, hills and forests did not meet with the injurious things and the hill-sprites; monstruous things and water-sprites did not meet with them [to do them injury]. Hereby a harmony was secured between the high and the low, and all enjoyed the blessing of Heaven. . ."

A Variety of Ceremonial Vessels

The Jia tripods are vessels for heating or serving wine. The one to the left is decorated with an animal mask (height 26 cm.) and comes from the excavations of Zhengzhou. The one in the middle is a Jia from the early Anyang period and the one to the right is a tripod with two upright elements in the form of a phoenix (height 41 cm.) from the late Shang dynasty, discovered in the excavations of Hejia, Qishan district, Sha'anxi province.

Opposite: The rectangular ding (cooking vessel) is the most important bronze artefact of the early Shang period. Two were discovered in 1974 in the excavations of Zhengzhou, Henan province. They are similar in form and decoration and have upright handles, a rectangular body in the form of a ladle, cylindrical feet and taotie mask motifs and studs (height 100 cm., weight 86.4 kg.).

53

Although they did not use the western lost wax method (which only appeared in China at about the beginning of our era) but the more complex one of proto-porcelain moulds, Chinese founders were not slow in greatly increasing the complexity of the animal motifs which decorated the vases. It would be tedious to review all the kinds of vessels – there are about fifty different types – and utensils which gradually appeared, partcularly from the fifteenth century BC onwards. However, some of the stylized motifs are worth describing, since they will, with certain variations, appear for almost a millennium. Firstly, the wolverine mask, the *taotie*, with immense eyes, sometimes unrecognizable because of the stylization, the *feng* phoenixes or the *long* dragons with or without paws, in striking postures. These fantastic masks are covered in linear motifs of clouds, lightning, scales – patterns of interlacing which appear to have had votive significance.

Detail of the decoration of the zun *wine container illustrated on the following page.*
Following pages: *Two wine containers; on the left, a* zun *decorated with the* taotie *motif, found in the excavations of Lingbao, Henan province; on the right, a* you *of the late Shang dynasty.*

54

ZHOU DYNASTY

11ᵀᴴ-4ᵀᴴ CENTURY B.C.

The victory of the Zhou over the Shang in 1027 BC was the victory of better organized noble families over less well organized ones, it was no longer a case of war against backward barbarians. Like their victory, their supremacy over the Central Plain for five centuries brought better social organization and a consolidation of political insitutions. Writing developed at the same time as the need for the codification of the rites, and this was reflected in longer, more detailed inscriptions on bronzes or in the later (its final version only dates from about the fourth century BC) *Zhouli* or Ritual of the Zhou, a compilation of the administrative traditions of this period. Several passages give an idea of the variety and precision of this code. Here, by way of example, are the duties of the Official in connection with the *zun* and *yi* vases:

"He is responsible for placing the six *zun* vases, the six *yi* vases. He indicates how one should draw them; he distinguishes their use and their contents. When one offers the *zei* sacrifice in the spring and the *yue* sacrifice in the summer, one uses for the libations *yi* type vases, known as the cock vase and the bird vase. For the first service of the morning, he employs two vases of single colour and of the *zun* form. For the second offering he employs vases of the same form but decorated with figures, With these various vases, there are *lui* vases from which the officers drink at the invitation of the sovereign. . . In general, at intermediate sacrifices between those of the four seasons, such as the sacrifice of retrospective meditation and the sacrifice of the visit to the court, he uses the *yi* vases known as the vase of the tiger and the vase of the great monkey. Both of these have a stand. For the service of the morning, he employs two large *zun* vases. For the second offering (the second meal), he uses two *zun* mountain vases. . ."

The *Zhouli* also provides us with information on the developments of the technology of alloying metals in its chapter "Workers who work metal":

"There are six proportions for the use of metal. When one divides the metal into six parts, and tin replaces one of these parts, one has the proportion for bells and pots. When one divides the metal into five parts, and tin replaces one of these parts, one has the proportion for large and small axes. When one divides the metal into four parts, and tin replaces one of these parts, one has the proportion for lances and pikes. . . When one divides the metal and tin in half, one has the proportion for metal mirrors."

The bronze mirrors referred to here are another mine of information for scholars on the cosmological ideas of ancient China, because their backs are decorated with numerous motifs reflecting these ideas. Still in the field of technology, considerable progress was made in the building of towns: the appearance of walled towns, and in architecture, the first tiled roofs. This was also the period when the first wells were drilled.

At the end of the eighth century the Quanrong tribe attacked Gaojing, the capital of the Zhou, forcing the dynasty to move east.

This *zun* vase (*vessel for alcoholic drinks*) depicts a bull. The extended tongue forms the spout and the entwined tail the handle. The lid is in the form of a tiger ready to spring. These realistic images form a significant variant on the similar vases in the form of birds and mythical animals from the late Shang and the early Zhou. (*height 24 cm., length 38 cm., weight 6.9 kg.*).

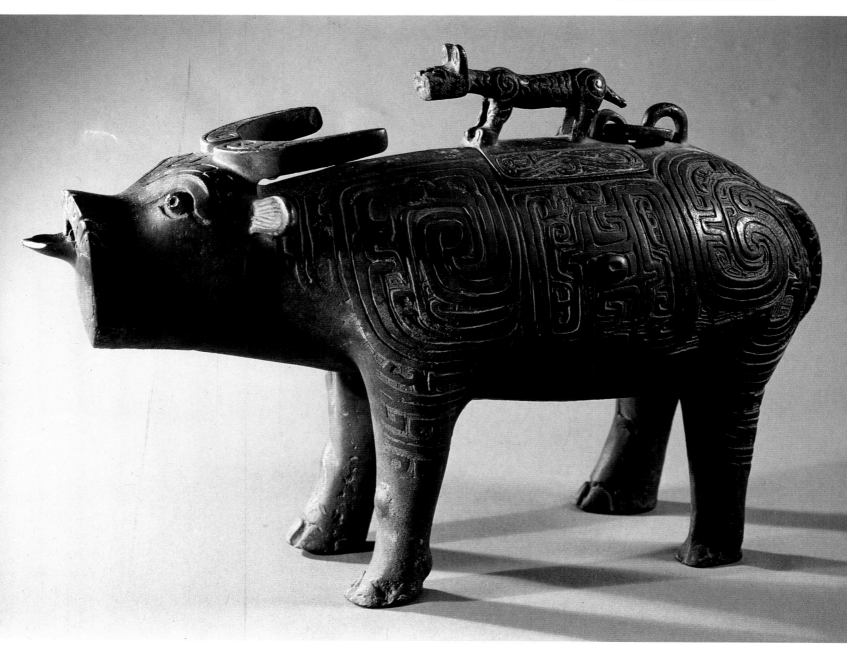

A gong vessel with a lid in the form of a giraffe's head, with a small dragon between the horns. The whole body is decorated with phoenix motifs.

A bronze ornamental figurine (height 11.2 cm.). Opposite, below: A square yi (a container for alcoholic drinks; height, 38.5 cm., weight 12.8 kg.), with a lid in the form of a palace roof, on which is incised an inscription identifying it as one of the ceremonial vessels which Tianshi had made for his dead father Riji.

62

Left and below: *A* gui *vessel made for Bo Zhong with an inscription which celebrates the feats of arms, in particular the liberation of 114 men captured by the enemy.*

A yi vessel (height 20.5 cm., weight 3.85 kg.) which bears a particularly long inscription. It says, in short: "In the month of March of the given year Count Yangfu declared a cowherd guilty of breaking his vows and of having falsely accused his master, demanding that he receive a thousand lashes and be condemned to death. Subsequently he only received 50 strokes and a fine."

Below: A three-legged bird with scale motif on its neck.

Left: *A hu vase made for Ji Fu. The inscription records that Ji Fu obtained a decoration in the Palace of the West.*

Below: *The most typical example of a late Zhou bronze, with a handle in the form of a dragon and a lid in the form of a vulture, inside which is the inscription "made for Tuo" (height 37.5 cm., weight 4.6 kg.).*

He vessel (height 29 cm.) with an inscription recording a sale of land during the reign of King Gong of the Zhou dynasty.

KINGS AND PRINCES AT WAR

This period is known as the Spring and Autumn era, until 475 BC, and subsequently as the Warring States era, until the end of the third century. However, so far as political institutions are concerned, there is no clear break between these two periods in ancient China. The first term is based solely on the existence of the *Spring and Autumn Annals* of the principality of Lu in Shandong. These *Annals* are traditionally attributed to Confucius.

THE WARRING STATES PERIOD

Metal working attained a high degree of refinement during this period, as the exquisite inlaid items testify.

It was during the Spring and Autumn and the Warring States eras that iron began to be cast in China and tools made from this metal began to be used. Ingots, an iron ball and an iron sword have been found in various tombs from this period. The sword had a carbon content of 0.5-0.6 per cent and displayed the marks of repeated forging — it is the first such sword ever discovered. A *ding* cauldron found with the sword was of cast iron and shows that in this field too China was two centuries ahead of Europe.

Recently, in the district of Daye, Hubei, a copper mine and foundry has been discovered. The excavation work has concentrated on two pits and eight furnaces. The galleries and vertical furnaces which have been excavated display an advanced knowledge of the processes of extracting and casting copper, side by side with the familiarity with and the high technical level achieved in the working of bronze.

In the course of this period there was a clear development in the workshops which produced bronze objects, ceramics, jades, bone and stone artefacts and a degree of regional specialization appeared. The state of Chu, for example, was known for its lacquers and its iron weapons, the central plains were responsible for some highly sophisticated objects incorporating gold and silver inlay, whilst the lower Yangzi valley produced the most advanced glazed ceramics.

During this period of expansion and specialization, as well as feudal fragmentation, a host of capitals and other cities arose. In the years following the foundation of the People's Republic Chinese archaeologists have been busy working on and excavating a host of cities.

The Wei tomb unearthed in 1950 in the province of Henan was the first large-scale excavation project following the foundation of the New China. More highly important finds have been made in numerous other tombs, the most recent being those of the state of Zhongshan in the district of Pingshan, Hebei and that of the Marquis Yi of the state of Zeng in the district of Suixian, Hubei.

The inscriptions on vases from this period are of considerable interest in that they provide information not contained in the annals – for example, the genealogies of the kings of Zhongshan and the events of the struggles between the states of Yan, Qi and Zhongshan. The funerary system in Zhongshan displays similarities with that of the Zhongyuan region from the same period and the inscriptions on the bronzes reflect the strong influence of this culture.

The excavations in May 1978 of the tomb of the Marquis of Yi at Leigudun, three km. north-west of the capital of the district of Suixian, Hubei, have made it possible to fix the position of the state of Zen, which up until then had been shrouded in mystery. The inscriptions on the bronzes suggest a close relationship with the neighbouring state of Chu. The Marquis Yi received a gift of a set of ritual bronzes from the King of Chu and the princes (with

Detail of a bronze basin.

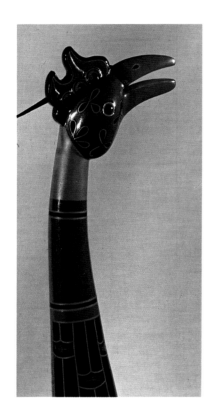

At Jinancheng, a city of the Chu state, a large quantity of bamboo, lacquer and wooden objects have been unearthed.

the official title of Lingyi) and nobles concerned themselves personally with the funeral.

More than 7,000 objects have been removed from the tomb of Marquis Yi, which dates from 433 BC or a little later. The most remarkable of these objects were various musical instruments: a series of 64 *Bian Zhong* bells and a large *Bo Zhong* bell were found intact and still hanging from their supports. The rear of each bell bore an inscription indicating its temperament, the names of the individual tonal systems and information which related the musical notation used in the state of Zeng with that current in the states of Chu, Zhou, Qi, Jin and others.

Altogether, the bronzes in Marquis Yi's tomb total no less than 10 tons and they included two *fou* vessels 1.3 metres high which each weighed 300 kilos. From 1951 onwards a group of Chu tombs have been explored at Changsha in Hunan province by the Institute of Archaeology of the Chinese Academy of Sciences. Beginning in the 60s excavations were carried out at Jinan, the capital of the Chu state and archaeologists from the Provincial Museum of Hubei discovered the portal north-west of the walls and the site of a palace. In recent years extensive study of the area stretching from the middle reaches of the river Changjiang to the valley of the river Juzhanghe west of the Changjiang and Hanshui has yielded numerous discoveries bearing on the question of the origin of the Chu culture. At Jinancheng, north of the district capital of Jangling in Hubei, there are walls of compressed earth, roughly square in shape and still in good condition. Around the city are scattered various Chu tombs. Highly complex in structure, they are generally covered by a tumulus and subdivided by wooden partitions. Each tomb contains two or three coffins. The variety of forms and the elaborate ornamental motifs suggest that the art of lacquer flourished in the state of Chu.

A Chu tomb at Wangshan, seven km. north-west of Jinancheng, has revealed an array of more than 700 funerary objects, including bamboo sticks on which were recorded divinations and sacrifices made by the occupant of the tomb, an engraved and painted base and a large brooch inlaid with gold and silver.

Amongst the finds from the Chu tombs of Wangshan was the famous bronze sword of Gou Jian, king of Yue.

60.8 cm. long, this is decorated with bas relief lozenges and appears as if it has just been taken out of the furnace. Yue bronze swords were famous throughout China at this period and were exchanged as precious gifts between princes. In this particular case, King Zhao of the Chu state took the daughter of King Gou Jian of Yue as a wife and the sword was probably one of the wedding gifts. It was found in the tomb of a noble and loyal servant of King Zhao, who was probably given it by the monarch himself.

In the transition between the Spring and Autumn era and the Warring States period, the social changes are reflected in the structure of tombs and in the array of objects buried in them. The ritual vessels (primarily the *ding*), which were the prerogative of royal and noble tombs give way to an increasingly large number of precious objects and the vessels themselves begin to be found in the tombs of commoners. For example in the tombs of the Chu state on the hill of Zhuogong, in the cities of Changsha and Chantaiguan and city of Xinyang, painted wooden artefacts greatly outnumber the ritual vessels which in the past symbolized the social rank of the nobility — a fact which suggests a marked change in the popular conception of wealth and honour compared to preceding ages.

In recent years archaeological excavations in the regions which belonged to the states of Zhongshan and Chu have found countless bronze, lacquer and jade artefacts.

In southern China, during the Spring and
Autumn era, the King of the state of Chu
brought the whole area of the upper and lower
reaches of the Yangzi river under his imperial rule.
In Hunan and Hubei provinces, Chinese
archaeologists have uncovered many sites; the objects
found in these sites have provided us with a wealth
of information about the Chu culture.

THE WARRING STATES PERIOD

5TH-3RD CENTURY B.C.

The entire period was marked by violent conflicts, internal struggles and attacks from outside. Here, general Yan Guang of the Zhou state is fighting the invasion of the Xiongnu nomads.

The institutions of the Zhou seemed very solid: at the top of a strict hierarchy there was a sovereign already known as the "Son of Heaven" (*Tianzi*), since he claimed to hold his powers from the rulers of the Natural Order. Privileges linked to each rank, ritual sacrifices attuned to the importance of the charge or the fief were more effective than arms in welding together an increasingly centralized state. Gradually, however, the principalities bordering on the Royal domain in the valley of the Wei began to cause problems and the Zhou were slowly reduced to acting as arbitrators between the local Lords, who increased in power and pressed home their attacks on all sides. By the end of the eighth century, after moving their capital a little further down the valley of the Yellow River, the Zhou were no more than a centrally situated state amidst other states. There then followed a period of military and political uncertainty which was to last a full five centuries, a period that was to be marked by alliances between states against other ones and by the emergence and disappearance of local powers.

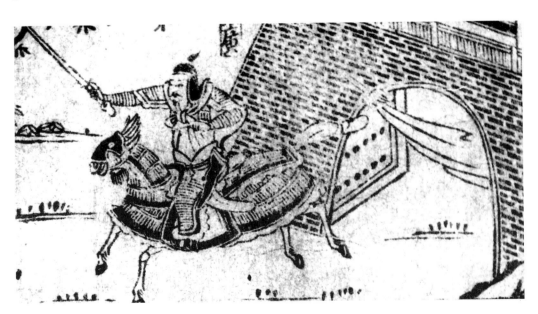

It was this state of rivalry between the Chinese states of the Central Plain which was to do most to bring them together both in terms of their institutions and also in their ways of life. Several cultural events contributed to this. The

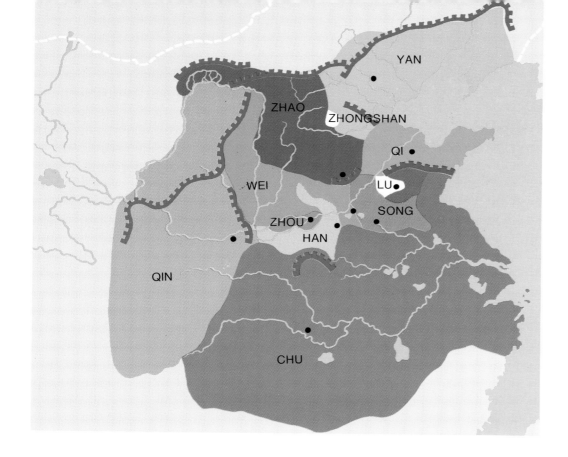

The complexity of the strategies adopted by the local sovereigns of the period recall Chinese chequers. As the following passage from the Zhanguoce chronicle (Memoirs of the Warring States) illustrates:
"Marquis Wen of Wei asked Zhao for right of way through Zhao to attack Zhongshan. Zhao was about to refuse when Zhao Li said: 'That would be a mistake! If Wei attacks but cannot take Zhongshan she will be exhausted by the attempt, while Zhao will become the stronger. If Wei takes Zhongshan she will never be able to control the peace across the entire country of Zhao, which will mean that the country obliged to use troops will be Wei but the one gaining territory will be Zhao. You would do best to allow passage... Zhao expects to profit by it and so will recall their troops. It would be best for your majesty to give them right of way and convince them that you can do nothing else'."

appearance of iron, about 500 BC, and its gradual adoption for agricultural implements, linked to the improvement in irrigation and agronomy in general, immediately led to a marked increase in production and in the well-being of the peasants. All this increasing wealth was reflected in luxury objects set in gold or silver, in the wider distribution of lacquer, once the preserve of the elite, amongst the moneyed classes. The working of jade, glass, weaving and, in general, all objects made by craftsmen experienced a tremendous surge; the bronzes became less heavy, less elaborate in their forms, whilst their motifs became scarcer or more figurative. Architecture grew more sophisticated, and the houses of the prominent personages in a town were roofed with tiles moulded with animal or stylized motifs.

The lives of the principalities gradually became organized around the capital or the major local centres, where the aristocracy gathered and a ruler minted money, despatched officials to more and more heavily administered regions and governed his kingdom. The towns, which grew more or less powerful, depending upon the circumstances, were

Restored terrace at Handan (Hebei), which is said to have been buit by Wu, King of the state of Zhao.

surrounded by thick fortifications of compressed earth which could be several miles long. Further fortifications were built little by little on the borders of zones of influence in order to ward off the attacks of envious neighbours. Finally, others were begun over stretches running for hundreds of miles in the northern regions of modern Shanxi and Hebei as protection against the populations of north-west China and the nomadic herdsmen, who gradually became formidable horsemen. Many of these northern fortifications were restored and linked together by the First Emperor to form part of the Great Wall.

Local differences did exist, even within the principalities of the Central Plain, for example between the maritime regions such as present-day Shandong, and the Hubei of the Chu or Shenxi, land of the Qin, who were still barbarians. However, the geographical position and the different forms of the economies of the peripheral principalities did not prevent their historical destinies from converging and nor did it prevent them from developing culturally in the same way. All these peoples were settled and not nomads of the steppe; in addition, the circumstances of war often led them to be imbued with a neighbouring local culture and little by little forged a solid basis for the Chinese identity: acknowledgement of the value of rites, of beliefs, political institutions and a system of writing. The spirit of each principality, however, so profoundly fashioned the Chinese mentality that even today every Chinese man insists on his place of origin.

The oldest example of painting on silk so far found in China was discovered in a Chu tomb at Changsha and depicts the occupant of the tomb astride a dragon whilst ascending to heaven after his death.

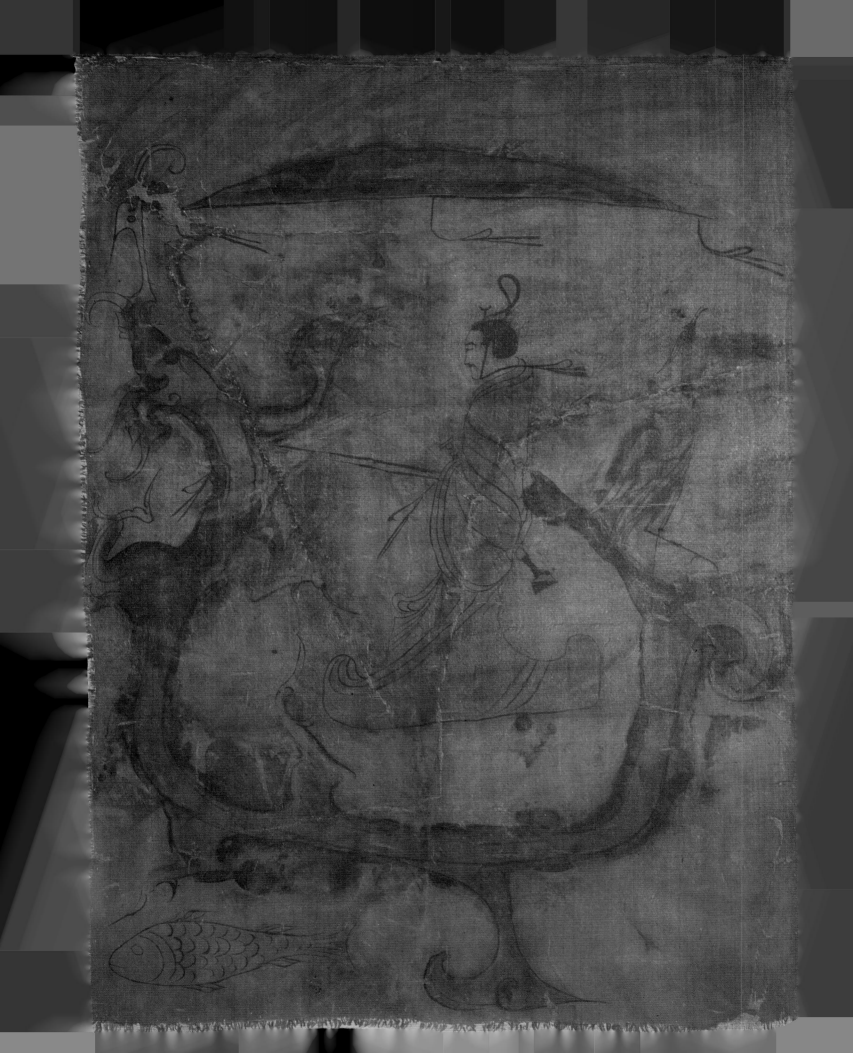

Precious Lacquers and Historical Documents of the Chu State

Tomb 1 of Tianxingguan, in Chu territory, excavated in 1978 still contained, after having been plundered several times over the centuries, more than 2,500 widely differing objects. Right: A drum support in polychrome lacquer in the form of two phoenixes which rest on two outstretched tigers.

Opposite: A splendidly made lacquer spoon (length 13.3 cm.) with an inscription which states that it was produced in the state of Chu.

The tombs excavated at Yunmeng, Hubei province, have yielded numerous artefacts typical of the state of Chu. The territory was conquered by the Qin in 279 BC and became one of its prefectures. Tomb 11 at Shuihudi contained the objects illustrated on these pages. The bamboo strips (totalling over 1,100 pieces) bear the codes in force under the Qin dynasty. The illustration is of a document of the Prefect Deng of Nanjun in the twentieth year of the reign of Qin Shi Huang (227 BC).

Below: *A cylindrical* zhi *wine cup with a ring-shaped handle (height 11 cm., diameter 12.5 cm.) in polychrome lacquer.*

Above: *A lacquer box (height 18 cm.) black inside, red on its outer surface, decorated with stylised phoenixes, clouds and geometric elements.*

HUBEI

"What agitation in the
autumn wind:
The waves of Lake
Dongting heave, the
leaves fall from the trees.
On the white sedges, my
gaze runs here and there;
In the black which stretches
out, I have a meeting with
beauty."

Before falling into the hands of the powerful Qin state in 277 BC, modern Hubei was the centre of the Chu kingdom. The name of this province means north of the lake, and refers to the maze of lakes which form Lake Dongting, which, together with the middle Yangzi, give this southern province a distinctive, misty appearance. Centuries later, it was this which was to influence the wash techniques of the landscape painters.

However, the kingdom of Chu also differed from the "central kingdoms" (Jin, Wei, Zhou) in other respects. It was less homogenous, its population of fishermen and hunters maintained a strong shaman tradition, where beliefs developed which may have had little in common with those of the Yellow River region, or the neighbouring states of Wu and Yue, on the lower Yangzi. There is more information concerning such matters during the Han period, thanks to the discoveries at Mawangdui, near Changsha in Hunan, which are discussed later. In any case, it is known that during the Warring States period the bounteousness of the region helped it develop a prosperous economy, although, even in this sphere, the region displayed unusual features, cowry shells were used for money, whereas all the other states had adopted currencies based on blades of knives or spades or even, at this early date, pierced discs. In daily life, lacquered utensils were extensively used and the warm, damp climate of Hubei offered excellent conditions for their preservation.

It was not solely economic prosperity which made the kingdom of Chu so full of life. It also benefited from its relative peace, which it owed to its out-of-the-way position and the difficulty that its extensive patchwork of lakes and water courses posed to an invader.

Some of the archaeological discoveries that have already been made in Hubei reflect this magnificence and one cannot doubt that future discoveries will confirm this, despite the adverse effects of the region's humidity on the condition of the tombs.

Precious Relics
of a Barbarian Civilization

The remains of the city of Lingshou, the capital of the state of Zhongshan, and of the tombs of its princes have been found in the district of Pingshan, Hebei province.

A good example of assimilation by barbarian tribes (in this case the Di) of Chinese customs and institutions is provided by the Kingdom of Zhongshan, a small principality, situated mainly in modern Hebei and then surrounded by the powerful Kingdoms of Qi in Shandong, Yan in northern Hebei and Zhao in southern Hebei. From historical sources this state was officially founded in 414 BC and was destroyed by its neighbour Zhao nearly two centuries later in 296.

Right: *Bronze fittings for a tent: pegs and the top of the central post.*

Opposite: *Jade figurines of ladies with the characteristic ox-horn head-dress and tight-sleeved garments. The figurine with the hair gathered up on the top of the head is of a child.*

Right: *Pierced topaz pendant with three dragons encircling the central ring.*

82

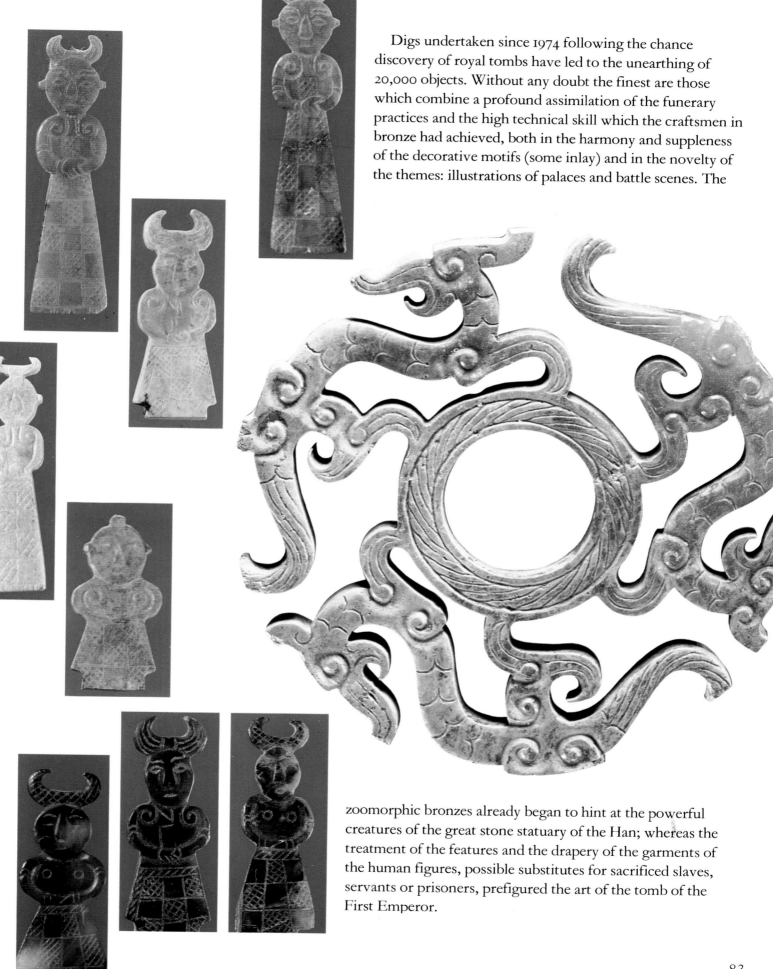

Digs undertaken since 1974 following the chance discovery of royal tombs have led to the unearthing of 20,000 objects. Without any doubt the finest are those which combine a profound assimilation of the funerary practices and the high technical skill which the craftsmen in bronze had achieved, both in the harmony and suppleness of the decorative motifs (some inlay) and in the novelty of the themes: illustrations of palaces and battle scenes. The

zoomorphic bronzes already began to hint at the powerful creatures of the great stone statuary of the Han; whereas the treatment of the features and the drapery of the garments of the human figures, possible substitutes for sacrificed slaves, servants or prisoners, prefigured the art of the tomb of the First Emperor.

Right: *A flat hu vase (height 45.9 cm.) with two loops on the neck and three rings on the lid. After 2,300 years it was found to contain wine.*
Far right: *A black pottery ding tripod (height, 41 cm.).*
Below: *A pen bowl (height 46.8 cm., diameter 60 cm.) inside which, on a small column, there is an eagle ready to take flight.*

Opposite: *A square hu vase (height 45.4 cm.), with a continuous geometric encrustation.*

Support for a screen in the form of a
gold and silver inlaid animal (height
21.5 cm.). The end of the panel was
fitted in the upright.
Opposite: Winged dragons with silver
inlay (height 45.4 cm.).

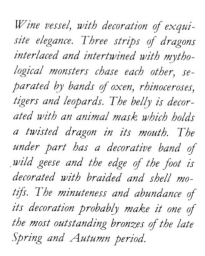

Wine vessel, with decoration of exquisite elegance. Three strips of dragons interlaced and intertwined with mythological monsters chase each other, separated by bands of oxen, rhinoceroses, tigers and leopards. The belly is decorated with an animal mask which holds a twisted dragon in its mouth. The under part has a decorative band of wild geese and the edge of the foot is decorated with braided and shell motifs. The minuteness and abundance of its decoration probably make it one of the most outstanding bronzes of the late Spring and Autumn period.

THE TOMB OF THE FIRST EMPEROR

"At the beginning of his enlightened reign, he reorganized the State, punishing the tyrants beyond the borders of Qin;
His increasing power made the edges of the world tremble and the six princes collapse;
Then he unified everything under Heaven, driving out evil and halting all war.
Shining is the virtue of the Emperor! He governs the world by means of his constant efforts.
He determined for every thing its due meaning and the way it should be written."

Sketch of the mound of Qin Shi Huangdi, with the notes of the American explorer W. E. Geil, who was one of the first to obtain precise information about it.

In March 1974, whilst digging a well in the district of Lintong, Sha'anxi, some peasants accidentally uncovered large numbers of terracotta fragments. Subsequent excavations by archaeologists established that the finds came from the tomb of Qin Shi Huang, the First Emperor of the Qin dynasty and this led to one of the most extraordinary archaeological discoveries ever made.

Born in 259 BC the future First Emperor ascended the throne at the age of 13. The young king then defeated and subjugated the six states to the east of his kingdom, decreeing the end of the Warring States period and consolidating for the first time China as a political and cultural entity subject to a centralized administration.

Historical documents state that work on Qin's tomb began as soon as he ascended the imperial throne and that it was still not finished at his death — it was in fact finished two years later by Hu Huai, his son and heir. The enormous complex required a total of 38 years work and some 700,000 labourers.

The tomb lies 24 km. east of Xi'an, on the northern bank of the river Wei, north-east of Mt. Lishan. The imperial mausoleum is covered by a 47 metre high tumulus and the remains of inner and outer surrounding walls have been found, one forming a rectangle, the other a square, as well as traces of various buildings and palaces. Three pits containing a terracotta army are clustered 1500 metres from the eastern wall and cover a total area of 20,000 square metres. The thousands of life-size soldiers arranged in battle formation face east in order to repulse any invader and were intended to protect the entrance to the emperor's tomb. Just as during his lifetime, Qin maintained an enormous army to protect Xianyang, his capital, so an impressive imperial guard had to surround and protect him in death. The discovery of a fourth pit suggests that the complex was still incomplete when the Qin dynasty fell.

The pits are five to seven metres below ground level and the original wooden structures which once enclosed them were destroyed, probably in the violent years which ended his domination. Pit 1 is rectangular and measures 210 metres from east to west and 62 metres from north to south. It contains more than 6,000 figures, with three rows of archers and crossbowmen at the front, armoured infantry in the centre and at the sides and behind these, three rows, in alternate ranks, of horsedrawn chariots and infantry. Finally, the rear is brought up by a row of archers facing outwards.

The warriors and horses are made of coarse grey clay, fired at high temperature. They were not made from moulds, but were modelled individually. Heads, arms and torsos of warriors were fashioned separately, then joined with clay strips. The hollow heads and torsos were support-

The life-sized figures of the underground army were surprisingly well preserved when they were discovered.

ed by solid clay legs.

Pit 2 lies 25 metres north of the eastern tip of pit 1, measures 96 metres east to west and 84 metres north to south and mainly contained chariots, cavalry and infantry. On the left front of the formation there are eight columns of archers, surrounded by 172 archers on foot, positioned to repulse an attacking enemy, alternating with kneeling soldiers. South of this formation there are eight columns of eight chariots, each being drawn by four horses, with a charioteer and two soldiers. In the centre of the group is a rectangular formation of 19 chariots arranged in two columns and escorted by 264 infantrymen. At the rear are eight saddled horses.

The third pit is 25 metres north west of pit 1 and 120 metres east of pit 2. It is U-shaped and is the smallest of the three, covering only 25 square metres. In the centre there is a covered carriage drawn by four horses and accompanied by an infantry escort. In the northern and southern chambers, 64 infantrymen bearing lances and facing inwards probably form a guard of honour. It appears that the pit may have been modelled on a military tomb. The terracotta soldiers seem to be of a higher rank and it is probably the headquarters of the army.

In the mid 70s, twelve Qin tombs were excavated in Hubei, an area occupied by the imperial armies in 229 BC. The lacquers and pottery that have been found reveal the influence of Qin culture. In tomb eleven Shuihudi, which dates from the thirtieth year of the reign of Qin Shi Huang, 115 strips of bamboo have been found and these provide valuable information on the military campaigns, the judicial system and the economy of the Qin.

In October 1980 two large bronze, covered chariots were excavated to the west of the Qin mausoleum. Drawn by four horses, each had a charioteer in an elaborate uniform with a sword at his side. They are about half life-size (328.4 cm. long and 104.2 cm. high). The highly detailed castings were covered with coloured pigments to increase their

The excavations of 1974 brought to light a complete funerary army guarding the tomb of the First Emperor. A total of almost 7,000 terracotta soldiers and 10,000 weapons. The columns of statues are arranged in three groups: the vanguard, the main body and the rearguard.

"As soon as the First Emperor became king of Qin,
excavations and building had been started at Mount Li,
while after he won the empire more than seven hundred thousand conscripts
from all parts of the country worked there.
They dug through three subterranean streams and poured molten copper
for the outer coffin, and the tomb was filled with models of palaces,
pavilions, and offices, as well as fine vessels, precious stones and rarities.
Artisans were ordered to fix up crossbows so that any thief breaking in would be shot.
All the country's streams, the Yellow River and the Yangzi
were reproduced in quicksilver and by some mechanical means made to flow into a miniature ocean.
The heavenly constellations were shown above and the regions of the earth below.
The candles were made of whale oil to ensure their burning for the longest possible time."

realism. The coverings of the horses and chariots were of gold and silver.

The discovery of these bronzes has brought into question many earlier hypotheses concerning the technological level achieved by the Qin in bronze working. The simple scale and sophistication of the imperial mausoleum necessitates a radical revision of the view of the period both by historians and archaeologists.

QIN SHI HUANGDI

221-210 B.C.

Jia Yi (201-169), the poet and statesman of the First Han makes this judgement on the iconoclastic first imperial dynasty in his work *Guo Qin lun* (The Faults of Qin):

"After it had become master of the whole empire and established itself within the fastness of the Pass, a single commoner opposed it and its ancestral temples toppled, its ruler died by the hands of men, and it became the laughing stock of the world. Why? Because it failed to rule with humanity and righteousness and to realize that the power to attack and the power to retain what one has thereby won are not the same."

The failure to value humanity (*ren*), the cardinal virtue of Confucianism, and the extremely rigid direction of the affairs of state were in fact constant features of the Kingdom of Qin from its emergence in 624 BC. In organizing in minute detail an authoritarian government from 221 onwards, the First Emperor was drawing extensively on the political tradition of his kingdom, which was heavily influenced by the Philosophy of the Legalist School and which included such major figures of that school as Shang Yang (fourth century). The iron hand who guided Qin to its apogee — and its fall — was a sort of Caesar with a large dose of Machiavelli, who was much concerned with symbolism and decorum. Although the legitimacy of his birth was somewhat doubtful, he had the good fortune both of attaining power in 246, when the Kingdom of Qin, which occupied the valley of the Wei, began to establish its military superiority; and also of being surrounded by like-minded ministers.

The *Historical Memoirs* of Sima Qian, completed at the beginning of the first century BC, provide detailed information on the life and work of this sovereign. The first years of his reign were marked by some promising military campaigns and above all, notes Sima Qian, by such auspicious natural phenomena as comets or by disasters (floods and locusts). After having bloodily put down some plots and rebellions, the man who was still only the King

94

". . . These opinionated scholars get together to slander the laws
and judge each new decree according to their own school of thought
opposing it secretly in their hearts while discussing it openly in the streets. . .
I humbly propose that all historical records but those of Qin be burned. . .
Those who in conversation dare to quote old songs and records should be publicly executed. . ."

of Qin already possessed the art of making those of his councillors who no longer served him pass for criminals. In about 237, one particularly bold councillor said of him:

"The King of Qin is a man with a prominent nose, large eyes, the chest of a bird of prey, the voice of a jackal; he has little kindness; his heart is that of a tiger or a wolf. While

The tumulus of the First Emperor, some 5 km. east of the capital of the district of Lintong, in Sha'anxi, rises to a height of 76 metres and numerous architectural fragments are scattered over a vast area around it.

he is bound, he finds it easy to make himself appear lower than the people; when he has obtained what he desires, it is as simple for him to devour them."

The sovereign was served by good strategists and bold generals; his campaigns often ended with the execution of tens of thousands of prisoners, a fact which had the advantage of discouraging any subsequent desire to rebel. It did not take him long to be master of China. He sent the best of his administrators to the new territories, taking care to place those of his relatives or children who had not been assassinated on his orders amongst them. Then he addressed his minister Li Si in these terms:

"I who am so unimportant, I have led armies to punish the rebel princes and, with the help of the power dispensed by our ancestors, the six kings have received the punishment they deserved so well and the country has finally found peace. Unless a title is created for us, how may this work be known to posterity? Let us discuss the question of an imperial status."

He himself cut short the discussion of his ministers by calling himself Supreme Emperor in imitation of the ancient dynasties and assuming, after the manner of the last Zhou rulers, the emblems associated with the function of the emperor: his era was that of water, the imperial colour was black and the dynastic number six. However, there was more than a liking for old tradition, because the years which followed were a period of great progress towards political, economic and moral unification: census of lands and territories, elimination of books of a general, nontechnical nature (poetry, philosophy, history for example), execution of uncooperative scholars, unification of the currency (copper sapek), of writing (elimination of numerous variants of characters and the establishment of an official method of writing), and unification of weights and measure. Criminal and administrative laws were enacted which strengthened the puritanism of customs. The development of roads radiating out from Xian-Yang, the capital, accompanied by the demolition of the old walls between kingdoms, encouraged traffic and helped the supervision of the whole empire. At the same time the northern fortifications were joined together into the Great Wall in order to ward off invasions.

It is not suprising, given the centuries of political division, that this shock treatment did not survive its instigator.

The First Emperor died at 50 without having managed to find the drug which conferred immortality nor the isles of paradise which were said to be off the coast of Shandong. These two obsessions of his life reflect his megalomania, as does the unheard of pomp of his burial. However, it is more than likely that China would not have known so much power and stability in its institutions in the four centuries that followed if the First Emperor, tyrannical as he was, had never reigned.

The First Emperor rose to absolute power over the whole of China by means of corruption, assassination and force of arms; driven on by the cold determination to achieve his objective of founding a centralized state, with a currency, standardized weights and measures and a single legal code.

The Terracotta Army

A short distance from the tumulus three pits have been excavated which contained a powerful terracotta army. Work, begun in 1974, is still continuing to repair the damage caused by fires, raids and so on.

On the following pages: *Pit 1, which measures 210 metres from east to west and 60 metres from north to south and contains more than six thousand figures. The museum which has been established at the site is the largest underground military museum in the world.*

98

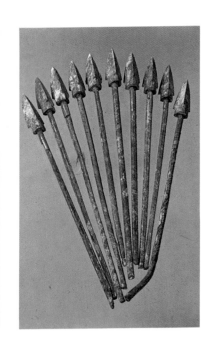

These kneeling warriors presumably held a bow. They form the front rank of the serried army and face outwards in order to protect it from any enemy. In the centre and at the ends of the row there is an infantry officer wearing armour and in the body of the army there are 38 rows alternating between horsedrawn chariots and infantry.

The bronze arrow heads and the loading mechanism for the crossbow are life size.

A Gallery of Figures,
a Variety of Hair-Styles

The terracotta figures are not from a single mould. They were produced in sections and then joined together and the details of the head and the folds of the garments were added later, special care being taken over the features which gave a unique identity to each of the figures. The hair was modelled with great realism in various different hair-styles: plaits joined together on the side of the head and fixed with a tie or covered by a hat tied under the chin.

The Chariots and Their Escort:
The Uniforms of the Officers and Soldiers

The charioteers are easily recognizable by their posture: arms held stiffly forward with closed fists as if holding the reins, with index and middle fingers separated to control the lines. All soldiers are clad in tunics, puttees and boots with square tips; the officers are distinguished by their massive bodies (the figure on the next page measures 1.95 m.), by their armour and by their double tunics.

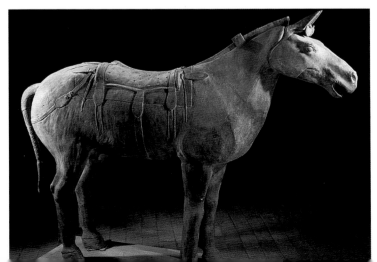

In 1980, six years after the discovery of the tomb of Qin Shi Huangdi, on the western side of the mausoleum, two well-preserved groups of bronzes of carriages and horses with their drivers were discovered.

111

The Splendid Bronze Coach

Following restoration the state coach has recovered all its splendour. It is about half life size (length 328.4 cm., height 104.2 cm.) and all the details are highly realistic. The door and the windows of the coach open and the furnishings of the coach and the horse are of gold. On the coach there is an officer with a hat and sword.

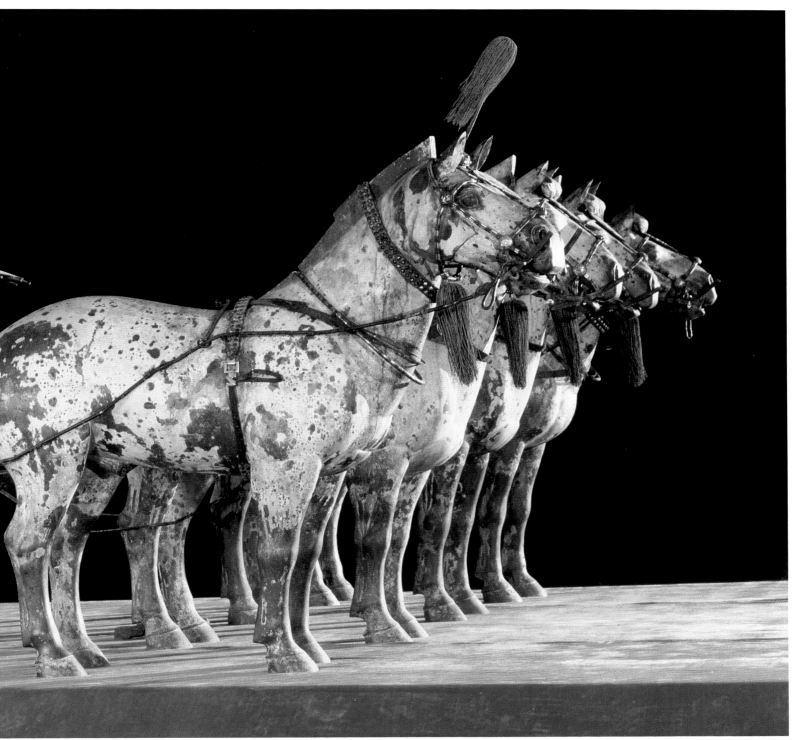

THE THOUSAND TOMBS

WESTERN HAN AND EASTERN HAN DYNASTY

"Chinese history is balanced on the figure ONE of our era, and the twin dynasty of the Great Han occupies this honourable point: the middle. . . The art of the Han is an art unknown to earlier or later times, unknown to our classical or barbarian West, an art which, until proof to the contrary, one can and must term purely Chinese, purely expressive of the ancient genius of China."

V. Segalen, *China, the Great Statuary*

With the coming of the Han dynasty the regional differences which still existed during the period of the Warring States disappeared in the course of the gradual fusion of the material cultures of the Han and those of the ethnic minorities of the neighbouring areas. It was at this time that the feudal empire consolidated itself. Over the last 30 years major excavations have unearthed numerous Qin and Han tombs and have catalogued the grave goods. Many of the tombs that have been discovered belonged to the members of royal or noble families.

The tomb of Prince Yan, discovered at Dabaotai near Beijing comprises a burial chamber known as "Huang Chang Ti Zhou" supported by more than 15,000 cypress slats 90 cm. long and totalling some 500-600 cubic metres of timber. The tombs of Liu Sheng, Prince of Zhongshan and his wife Dou Wan on the hill of Lingshan at Mancheng in Hebei and that of Liu Qingji, prince of Lu on the hill of Jiulong at Qufu, Shandong presented complex engineering problems since they had to be dug deep into the rock. Tomb 1 at Mawangdui was intended for Xing Zhui, wife of Li Cang, Marquis of Tai and Chancellor of the principality of Changsha at the beginning of the Western Han. This is a large tomb with two wooden partitions and four coffins. Tombs of local officials and army officers have been excavated in Inner Mongolia, in Gansu, Guangxi and in the autonomous region of Zhuang. A large number of important artefacts have been brought to light, including wall paintings, bronze chariots and horse figurines. They depict a multiplicity of subjects: figures, chariots, horses, dances, festivals, sacrificial rites and even stories and historical figures – providing a vivid and lively picture of social life at the time of the Han.

Exquisitely made figurine of a bird resting on a dragon (height 30 cm.).

The Mawangdui tombs, situated at the eastern edge of Changsha, were excavated between 1972 and 1974. The information that came to light confirmed that they were the tombs of Li Cang, the Marquis of Dai, appointed Chancellor of the principality of Changsha, his wife and his son: the entire family having been buried about 168 BC.

Tomb 1 was occupied by the Marchioness Xin Zhui and is a funnel-shaped pit with a ramp leading to the bottom. Four coffins, one inside the next, occupy a further wooden burial chamber measuring 6.7 by 4.81 metres and 2.8 metres high. The outer coffin is decorated with wonderful lacquered motifs: amidst the clouds which enfold its sides are the immortals and various mythical beasts. There were about 1400 burial objects, some of which (clothes, food, fruit and medicinal herbs) are enclosed in 48 bamboo boxes. There are 162 wooden statuettes, including court ladies and servants, musicians and dancers. The inventory of the objects is recorded on 312 strips of bamboo. One of the coffins is covered by a T-shaped *fei yi* ("flying cloak") on which are painted scenes of the supernatural, the earth and heaven.

Detail of the painted silk banner which covered one of the sarcophagi found at Mawangdui, 5 km. east of the city of Changsha, in western Han tombs.
Opposite: *The excavation of tomb 1.*

The body of the lady in the innermost coffin is well preserved. Her hair is still firmly attached to her skull, her skin elastic and her joints mobile. This is due to the acids in the coffin and its tight seal. Tomb 2 was plundered in the distant past and little remains of it, although the identity of its occupant is known from a number of seals. The son of Li Cang was buried in tomb 3 and it resembles the first one but is smaller. Particularly important are a score of silk books which were thought to have been irrecoverably lost. Maps of suprising accuracy and richness of detail provide evidence of the advances in the art of topography. One of them covers the modern province of Hunan and the adjacent areas of the provinces of Guangxi and Guangdong; another, measuring 98 by 97 cm. and drawn in black, red and blue, provides a detailed picture of the defences of Changsha, marking the new military encampments and the distances between the residential palaces, as well as the number of inhabitants. The weapons found in the tomb indicate that its occupant was a general.

The two, deep tombs discovered at Mancheng by a unit of the popular liberation army turned out to be those of Prince Jing of the kingdom of Zhongshan and his wife Dou Wan, who were buried between 113 and 104 BC. They are sited on the top of a hill 1.5 km. from the district capital of Mancheng, Hebei, and they are some 50 metres deep, with a vaulted ceiling and curved walls, vestibules, galleries, an access ramp and several chambers. These multi-chambered structures, which were derived from the dwellings of the living, constitute a significant advance over the single-chambered type prevalent at the beginning of the Han period. Similarly, the ritual practice of enclosing the prince in a nest of five coffins was abandoned. In these tombs there is simply an inner and an outer coffin. Finally, the fact that Liu Sheng and his wife occupied separate burial chambers in a single tumulus may be viewed as a precursor of the burial in connected chambers of the later Western Han. There were about 4,000 burial objects — the largest number being pieces of pottery and some of which were a continuation of the style of the Warring States whilst others displayed new forms and ornamental styles. The bronzes are quite exceptional. The figure of the palace lady holding a lamp, which comes from the palace of Ciangxin, the *boshan* incense burner with gold inlay, the *hu,* vase with inlaid and embossed decoration, are works of art of quite extraordinary beauty. Amongst the finds there were gold and silver acupuncture needles, a complete suit of iron armour, and two bronze supports and fittings for tents, the first ever

found in a Han tomb. The two occupants were clothed in jade garments; that of Liu Sheng comprised 2,498 jade tesserae of various shapes held together by gold thread passed through holes made in the four corners. One of the most important archaeological discoveries of recent years has been the strips of wood and bamboo bearing inscriptions that provide a wealth of information on the Han and Qin dynasties, coupled with the silk books of Mawangdui.

In the north west of Gansu (valley of the river Egina), investigators have excavated the remains of Han guard towers and garrisons. More than 20,000 strips of bamboo have been found. Most of these are official documents and books in which the tasks of the garrison soldiers and the farming activities of the region were recorded – documents and information which are of great value historically.

During the Han dynasty iron objects were produced and used on a wide scale. The government had a monopoly on casting dating from the time of the Emperor Han Wu Di and the remains of foundries have been excavated at Tieshenggou, Gongxian district, Henan between 1958 and 1959 and at Guxingzhen, Zhengzhou in 1975. Pits, furnaces, fuel and accommodation have been uncovered and testify to the advanced state of casting techniques at the time of the Han.

The remains of a boatyard dating from the Qin and Han periods were found in Guangzhou in 1974. The yard, which comprised a dockyard and a slipway, was capable of building several ships of 50 or 60 tons at a time. The flourishing trade and the good communications at the time created conditions that favoured shipbuilding.

So far as the artefacts of zones occupied by ethnic minorities are concerned, various objects were excavated in the winter of 1972 from the tombs of Xiongnu herdsmen in various districts of the autonomous region of Inner Mongolia. The finds include gold thread, necklaces and magnificent ornaments in the form of tigers, sheep, cattle, porcupines and so on – the animals which they would find on the pastures. The discoveries of the Xiongnu tombs in Liaon-

The army arranged in battle formation which has been unearthed at Yangjiawan, in Sha'anxi province, numbers thousands of figurines, which are smaller in size than those of the mausoleum of the First Emperor.

ing provide information that sheds new light on the culture and customs of these peoples. Excavations carried out on a group of tombs of the Dian tribe in Yunnan have brought to light various bronzes, including weapons, musical instruments, everyday articles and ornaments. The seal of the king of Dian, granted by the Emperor Han Wu Di at the institution of the Yizhou prefecture in 109 BC, has also been found. The excavated objects which date from the Warring States period and the beginning of the Han are very different from those of the plains and display marked Dian features. However, by about the middle of the Han period the influence of the plains is clearer. For example, the *ge* sword-axes and the *bian zhong* bells display similarities with the corresponding objects of the plains, whilst retaining specific characteristics in the details. In the transition from the Western Han to the Eastern Han, the objects generally follow Han style, reflecting the interweaving of the diverse culture and peoples within China.

Four seasons of excavations were undertaken at Shizhai-shan, 5 km. from the district capital of Junning, between 1955 and 1960. The 48 tombs which have been discovered contained more than 4,000 bronzes dating from the period of the Warring States to the Han dynasty. Subsequently, a further two thousand Shizhaishan type bronzes have been found scattered over 35 sites around Lake Dianchi.

This figurine forms part of the rich array of grave goods of a Han general, whose tomb has been found at Leitai, Gansu province.

The bronze vessels of the Dian area decorated with geometric motifs or with highly realistic cast figurines. A strong regional style is apparent both in the subject matter and in the casting. The human figures on the vessel lids are depicted in the act of making sacrifices, going hunting, paying tributes, herding and raising their livestock, eating and making love, etc. For example, the lid of a container for cowry shells which is only 30 cm. in diameter has a hundred figures crowded on it. Some celebrate a ceremony, others feed tigers and goad livestock, others still are feasting merrily, some are bustling about serving and others are offering sacrifices. Another, pierced example depicts a struggle between fierce beasts. Animal motifs abound: horses, cattle, sheep, tigers and peacocks, as well as mythical beings such as sphinxes and winged tigers. The thematic wealth and the variety of modelling mark all these artefacts as typical Dian products. All the Shinzhaisjan tombs are tumulus tombs and some contained red lacquered coffins.

Two discoveries of major importance were made among the Han tombs excavated in 1983. One is the imperial tomb in the state of the Southern Yue, the excavation of which began in August 1983. This is the largest stone tomb ever found south of the Nanling mountains. Archaeologists have uncovered a very large quantity of finds here. It lies inside the hill of Xianggang, 20 metres from the summit and comprises six chambers, three in front, three behind. It is 10.85 metres long, 12.43 metres across at its widest point and the ceiling is covered by large stone slabs, the largest of which (2.5 metres by 2.2 metres and 24 cm. thick) forms the ceiling of the front cell. The front cell and the rear, central one are sealed by stone doors. More than 1,000 funerary objects have been found here, the most important include over 500 bronzes, 200 jade items, bronze bells, stone bells, Nanyue style cooking vessels, Xiongnu style bronze plates with reliefs of fighting animals, a screen with a three metre bronze cornice and a bronze mirror. In the central, rear room an outer and an inner coffin were found, but the actual coffin and the skeleton of its occupant have disintegrated. The tomb's occupant was clad in jade garments and had six swords by his side. There were jade ornaments by his head and a necklace of jade pearls on his chest. Both above and below the garment there were dozens of jade *Pi* (ritual objects some 30 cm. in diameter with a hole in the centre). Nineteen gold seals were found, objects that have only rarely been found in Han tombs at other sites. The largest is a bracelet in the form of a dragon on which are incised the characters of the Emperor Wen, which confirms that the tomb's occupant was the second emperor of the Nanyue state. On the basis of historical documents, the Nanyue

The ethnic minority of the Dian flourished under the Han and produced bronzes and other artefacts with the typical features of the art of the steppes.

state was ruled by a separatist regime in the area south of the Nanling mountains for 93 years at the beginning of the Western Han dynasty. The discovery of the tomb has yielded important cultural information for the study of the economic and cultural development of this zone during the Qin and Han dynasties and has provided clues concerning the tomb of the first Nanyue emperor.

The other major discovery was the recent identification of Han tombs in the province of Shanxi. The discovery was made during open cast coal mining at Pingshuo. Over an area of 1.26 million square metres more than a thousand Han tombs have been identified, with more than 8,000 finds. The family tombs encompass all the types of Han tombs in their various stages over a span of 400 years, covering both the Western and Eastern Han dynasties. Most are small or medium-sized tombs and large ones are rare in the deposits of stone and coal.

Most of the burial objects that have been discovered are pieces of pottery, with a certain number of lacquers, jade artefacts, and wooden implements. Some finds, such as the glazed pottery (proto-porcelain), the bronze mirrors, the weapons and so on are out and out treasures.

The depiction of animals is a constant feature of the art of peoples of the steppe.

At Shuoxian, Shanxi province, more than a thousand Han tombs have been excavated near an open-cast coal mine. The finds they have yielded have been of great interest.

124

"Inside the town the roads and intersections are connected to each other and stretched far off, the gates and doorways of the streets and the portals numbered in their thousands. There are nine market squares arranged by merchandise and the roads are lined by shops leading to the markets grouped by the kinds of merchandise. Men do not return, carts do not advance, they fill the confines of the town and overflow to the suburbs. Along the sides there are hundreds of shops; the red dust kicked up on four sides mingles with the clouds and smoke. . . The knight errants of the town are like dukes and marquises, the merchants of the rows of shops exceed in prodigality the princesses of the Ji and the Jiang . . ."

WESTERN HAN DYNASTY

2ND–1ST CENTURY B.C.

The son of Qin Shi Huangdi, Er Shi Huangdi, (the Second Emperor) did not manage to maintain the ideological discipline imposed by his father and the empire collapsed in 207 BC, three years after the death of its founder, swept away by peasant revolts. It was a minor official, a certain Liu Bang who, backed by the peasantry, some years later assumed the Mandate of Heaven and founded the Han. Liu Bang had had an uncertain life and careers as diverse as inn-keeper and officer in the police when the peasant revolts which swept the Qin away left a power vacuum. There were numerous rivals for power but Liu Bang, by betraying his companion in arms Xiang Xu, had the luck of being the first to lead his armed band over the passes which commanded the valley of the Wei, the key to power. It was then 206 BC.

The first decisions of the new strong man of the Central Plain, who was installed in Chang'an (town of the "long quietude", modern Xi'an), involved the distribution of fiefs to his best officers and the founding in 202 of the Han dynasty, the name of the state which had brought him to power. Liu Bang inherited a centralized state with a solid administrative system and powerful means of supervision created by the First Emperor. He had the wisdom to touch nothing and to continue the Legalist tradition of the government. The Han State carried on unaided, all that was necessary was to make somewhat more moral a political power tainted by cruelty, to generate wealth, and restore the dignity of scholars and their role in cultural life and government. However, he happily made fun of the latter and their advice – it even being said that he pissed in their caps. Neverthless, he left them to develop Confucianist ideas which were eventually to have considerable influence on customs and government. Chang'an rapidly became a prosperous capital; it was to be the capital of China for two centuries. At the beginning of the Han dynasty, which was to rule almost without a break for nearly four centuries, Liu Bang took the name of Gaodi the "Exalted Emperor", so continuing the imperial tradition established by his bloody predecessor. He perpetuated by this act a Chinese political institution which would never be fundamentally challenged until 1911.

All that remained was to ensure the territorial power of the Han and this was done by immediately consolidating the Great Wall in the region of Gansu, then in Inner Mongolia and Manchuria. Hundreds of thousands of peasants, gradually replaced by soldiers and convicts were to bleach their bones for this immense work. Other major works were undertaken, canals were dug, roads extended, the dikes along the Yellow River strengthened (this did not prevent catastrophic floods and a change of course at the beginning of the first century BC).

But "the best form of defence is attack" was the view of the "Martial Emperor" Wudi, Liu Bang's fifth descendant. He reorganized the army and launched a series of attacks against the Xiongnu (probably the ancestors of our Huns) in Central Asia, beginning about 130 BC. These attacks were more than punitive expeditions because the emperor left military garrisons behind him linked by relays and signals as well as creating territories in the western parts of Gansu. To the north-west, he colonized Manchuria and a large part of modern Korea. To the south, he sent armies beyond the Yangzi to subjugate the Kingdom of Dian (Yunnan) and other local kingdoms up to the borders with Burma. All these military operations were accompanied by the settlement or eviction of populations sometimes numbering hundreds of thousands of individuals.

This sinification of the borders completed the territorial formation of China as it exists today. There then began to develop a Chinese sphere of influence, from Vietnam to Central Asia and Korea. Although local disparities existed and still exist in these frontier zones and even within the country, the way was now clear for such original Chinese concepts as the administrative system, the rites and writing to spread out over the whole of the Far East.

The grief of separation when the armies were levied or populations moved rapidly became a major literary theme; it occurs for example in the later passage from the *Wenxuan*:

"The frontier provinces have still not been pacified, you must follow the army, with your feathered arrows on your back,
The waters of the Liao have no limits the mountains of Yan are near the clouds – the river and region of the North. . .
We break branches of peach and cherry trees, we cannot bear to part.
I accompany my beloved son and my apron of silk is wet with tears."

HEBEI

The period of the Warring States brought the kingdom of Zongshan, in the modern province of Hebei, into the limelight. Invaded by its neighbour Zhao in 250 BC, this small state fell to the First Emperor shortly thereafter, in about 228. With the rise of the Han, it became an ideal fief for a member of the imperial family. As luck would have it, the tomb of a descendant of Liu Bang, the Prince Liu Sheng (155-113), brother of the Han Emperor Wudi, has been discovered there and it contains a considerable quantity of fine grave goods.

Some of the objects found in the burial chamber of Liu Sheng and his wife, whose chamber was beside his, have already been illustrated. As a group, these objects help us to understand the ideas of the Chinese people of this region concerning life after death. They form a complete house interior, with lamps of various forms, weapons (including iron swords, which were only just beginning to be made), acupuncture needles, bronze vases and basins, sometimes inlaid with gold. There is a bronze perfume burner decorated with a landscape that transports one in imagination to mountains and valleys whose bewitching beauty and miniature plants and animals inspired poets and conjured up halcyon days. This miniature world is reflected throughout the tomb. Everything needed for everyday life was present and, his soul having taken flight, the body of the deceased could satisfy his needs without difficulty. Similarly, the jade garment which clothed the deceased was intended to preserve his life, jade being endowed with numerous qualities in the Chinese pharmacopoeia, strengthening the *yang* principle of the body, it formed part of many elixirs aimed at prolonging life. It appears that the custom of dressing the dead in jade, which is a striking feature of the Han, reflected a deep interest of the society of the time, and the Emperor Wudi in particular, in magico-religious practices. Gold was endowed with numerous virtues and this is the reason why gold thread was used in such jade garments. However, as the texts tell us, honour to whom honour is due, the practice was exclusively reserved for rulers or the very highest strata of society. The custom of stopping up the orifices of a deceased person with jade objects or cowries does, on the other hand, seem to have been more widespread; its purpose being to improve the preservation of the body.

The walls of tombs in Han China were often decorated.

The rulers and nobles began to build their tombs years in advance and the craftsmen engaged on this work had plenty of time in which to paint or sculpt the bricks out of which the chambers, ante-chambers or corridors of the tombs were built.

The hill of Lingshan at Mancheng, Hebei province. Two tombs lying a hundred yards apart on its slopes have been excavated. These belonged to Liu Sheng, Prince of Jing of the Kingdom of Zhongshan, and his consort.

129

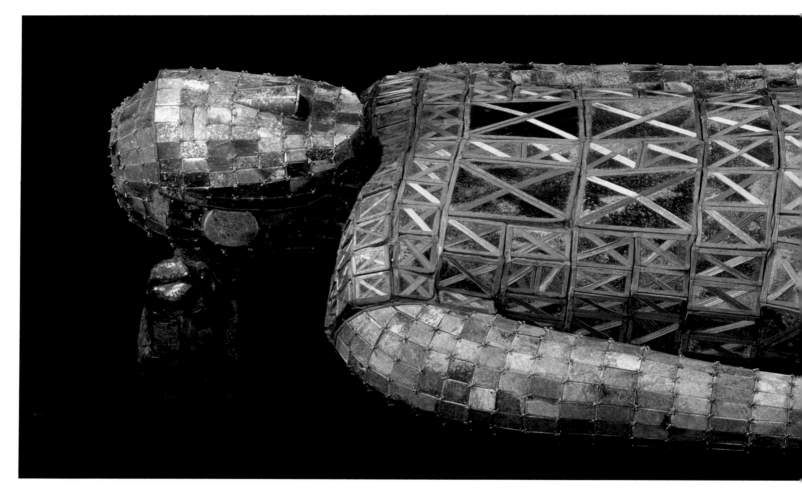

Numerous artefacts, including these pi *discs, have been found in other important Han tombs in the province of Hebei.*

Right: Pi *disc of white jade (height 30 cm., diameter 24.4 cm.) decorated with two dragons holding a cup, excavated from the Han tomb of Beilingtou, Dingxian district.*

Far right: A pi *disc of green nephrite decorated with hydras was excavated at Beizhuangzi, Dingxian district (height 22.5 cm., diameter 19.9 cm.).*

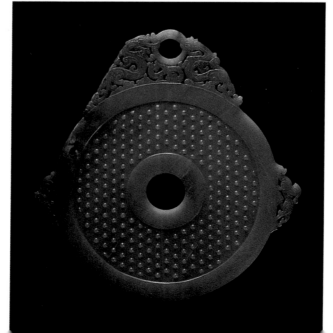

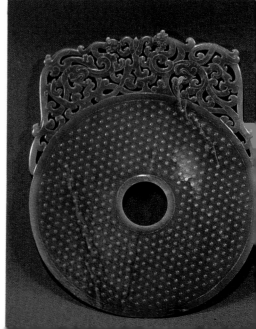

The rich array of objects in the two tombs includes jade pieces, bronzes and ceramics.

The jade garment of the Princess Tou Wan is, together with that of her consort Liu Sheng, the first complete example to be found. It is composed of 2,156 pieces of jade linked by fine gold thread and weighs a total of 700 grams. Jade, which was reserved for the

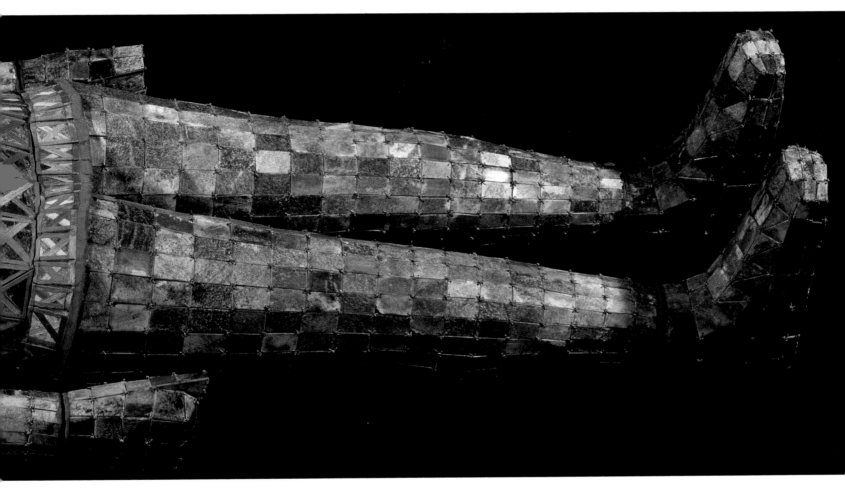

emperors and the nobility, was traditionally regarded as having protective powers. The upper part of the garment formed a sort of jacket in which the plates are wrapped in gilt ribbons. The head of the princess rests on a bronze pillow.

The painted terracotta pen bowl (height 13.7 cm., diameter 56.2 cm.) with bird decoration belongs to a group of twelve pieces, all decorated with different motifs. The colours and motifs mimic the effects of lacquer, a costly material which was replaced by less noble products, even in the richer tombs.

131

"The shining orchid-perfumed candles
Illuminate the flower-like faces which attend you;
Two times eight servants to stand at your bed head, who take turns in your service,
Charming young maidens of noble family far surpassing common servants
O, soul, return!. . ."

The lamp on the previous page comes, as the inscription shows, from the Changxin palace, where the empress mothers lived, and it was made between 173 and 159 BC. The sleeve of the maiden forms the hood of the lamp and the disc at the base may be turned to vary the direction of the light.

This ding *tripod (height 18.1 cm., diameter 17.2 cm.) is supported by three crouching bears.*

Below: *The bronze vase decorated with dragons with two bodies and flying clouds bears an inscription on its base which states that it originally belonged to a King of the Chu state.*

133

Above: *A bronze figure of a bird resting on a dragon (height 30 cm., weight 8.2 kg.). The plate of the lamp has three points.*

Above and opposite: *Figure of a bird with a jade disc in its beak, encrusted with turquoises. Remains of a red substance, possibly used as a cosmetic, have been found in the two side cups.*

134

An important tomb has been excavated at Dabaotai, near Beijing; plundered and burnt in the distant past, it has yielded more than 400 artefacts. The burial chamber measures 23.2 m. by 18 m. and was built from 500-600 cubic metres of wood. This type of wooden sarcophagus was only intended for use by emperors and this one was the first found in China.

In the entrance corridor of the tomb there were three coaches painted with coloured lacquer. This is the only example of a functional ancient carriage still in existence.

The grotesque figure opposite is a gilded bronze door knocker, whilst the powerful leopard on this page was probably a weight used for holding down the corners of a mat. From what is known of the customs of antiquity, the Han used to sit on the ground.

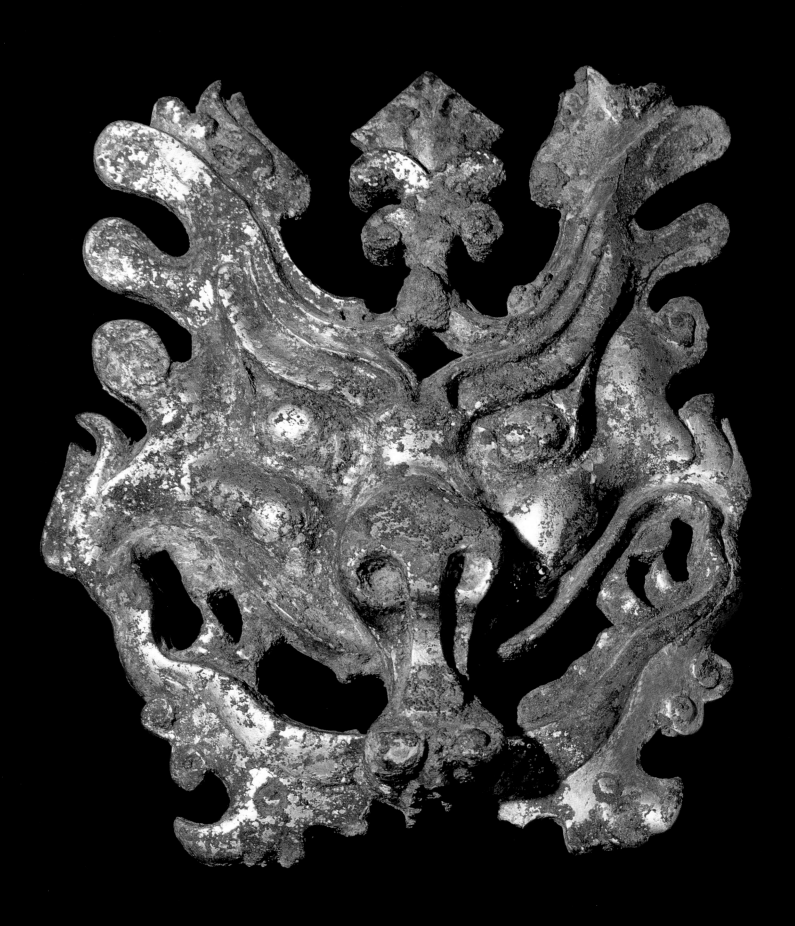

HUNAN

1,000 kilometres south of Hebei, the province of Hunan is far-removed from the China of the Yellow River and the basin of the lower Yangzi. As its name, which means south of the lake, suggests it lies south of Lake Dongting. Without being as out of the way as its neighbour Guangdong, it was for long the "country of the Chu" of the Warring States and it has always been very different in its traditions.

At the time of the Han, the realm of the Chu was still the purest heir of the ritualistic tradition of the Shang and divinatory practices were particularly strong. The geographical part of the *Book of the Han* which describes the customs in vogue in this region mentions that the inhabitants believe in sorcerers and demons and that the people follow all sorts of cults. They also venerated the souls of the deceased with a quite unusual fervour and the ceremonies incorporated practices that were probably extremely ancient. This is borne out by two burial sites which were uncovered in 1973 at Zitanku and at Mawangdui in the region of Changsha, the present capital of Hunan.

The banners which have been found draped over the coffins in the burial site of Mawangdui in the region of Changsha, the present capital of Hunan, are particularly revealing. Flying cloaks for the deceased in his ascent to heaven, which are decorated with cosmological and mythological scenes and ones connected with a belief in a journey into the world of paradise, provide a plethora of information. At the bottom one can see the world of earthly forces and the divinities connected with it; in the centre the paired dragons which are the mounts used in the ascent, criss-crossing within a ring of jade symbolizing heaven. Large numbers of these have been found in tombs of every period. Meanwhile, figures in prayer perform ritual sacrifices for the journey of the deceased to the beyond, phoenixes act as emissaries of the celestial powers who are depicted in the upper, more extensive part. Nine of the ten suns are present, as well as the mulberry tree which, according to an ancient text, grows in the valley of the rising sun.

These paintings suggest that Paradise is associated with Mt. Kunlun, a mythical site of obscure origin but which may be related to Mt.Meru the axial mountain of the Indians.

142

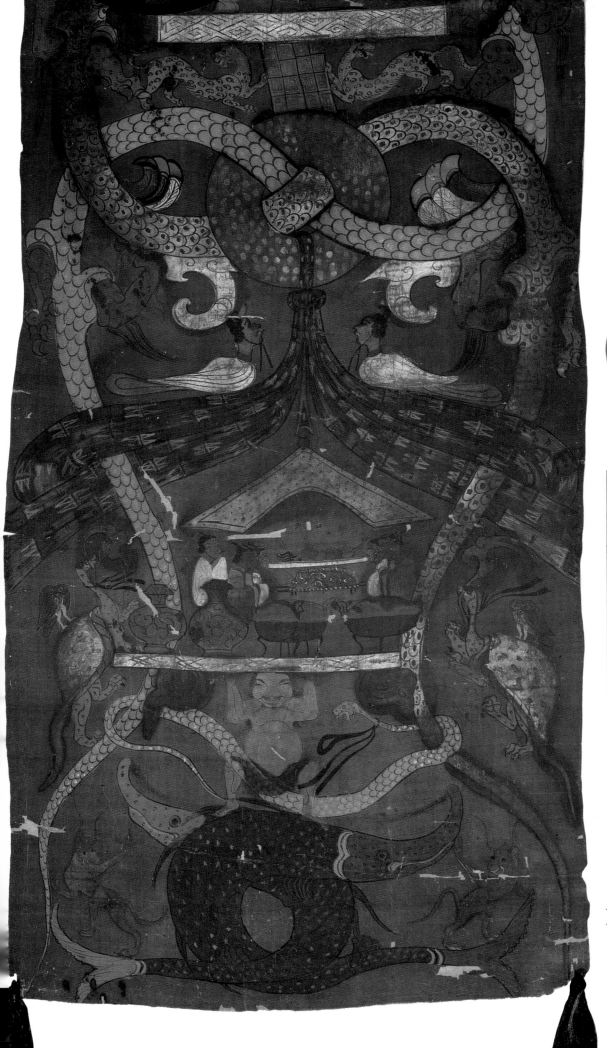

Following pages: *The riches of the tombs of Mawangdui include numerous silk manuscripts, such as a Treatise on the Planets (Xingjing), a page from which is illustrated here and which describes the movements of the planets and the comets. The wooden figurine (height 79 cm.) with carved facial features, wearing a tunic and hat and a silk garment decorated with lozenges, bears the inscription "chief of the servants" on the sole of its shoe.*

Many silk documents were discovered in tomb 3 at Mawangdui (near Changsha, Hunan), which dates from 168 BC. They included this roll on which are depicted clouds, stars and comets, as well as the symbols which are connected with them. Numerous astronomical, meteorological and astrological notes have been added for each of the 300 items which make up the work. Not all the texts can be deciphered because of

the poor condition of the backing. Nevertheless, one can, here and there, make out speculations concerning heavenly manifestations: "an emissary will arrive" or "the territory will expand" or "the war will break out". Unlike other divinatory practices, these oracles which draw their inspiration from the macrocosm seem to be addressed to the community rather than to individuals. The plethora of details on the form, nature and recur-

rence of astral events reveals the great extent of scientific knowledge in this field. However, astrology was one of the disciplines proscribed by the First Emperor and it is probable that, despite its scientific interest, this work would have been condemned 50 years earlier.

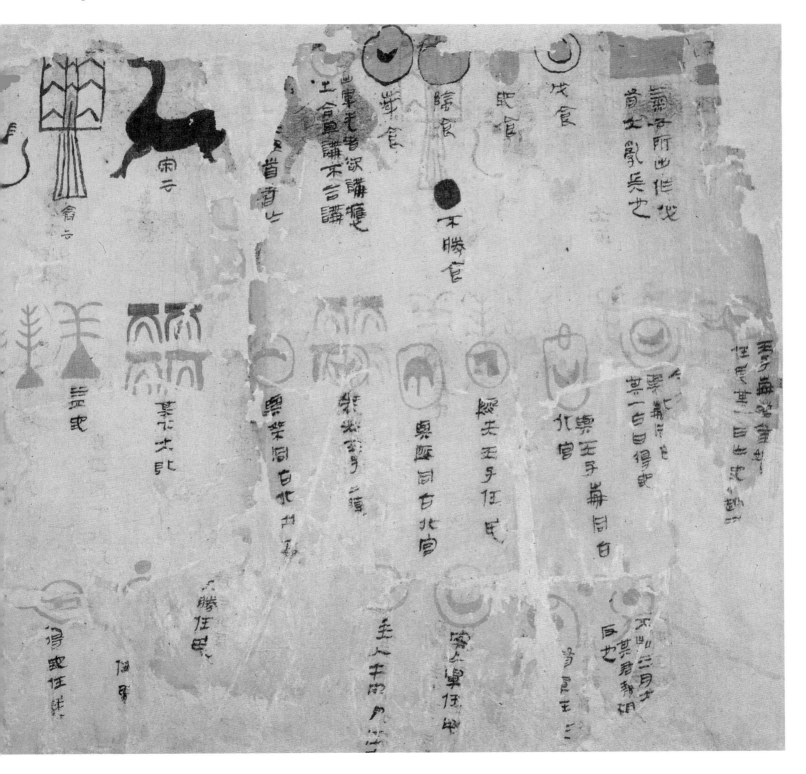

GUANGDONG

It is not possible to say, given the present state of archaeological excavations in this region, that Guangdong had reached a technological and cultural level comparable to that of its neighbour Hunan in the second century BC. The geographical and climatic conditions and the population were also different and it is unlikely that the ways of life or thought had much in common.

Guangdong is drained by a separate river system, that of the Xi, whose basin is extremely fertile and where hunting, and above all fishing, rapidly ensured the independence of the Guangzhon region from the more northerly parts of China. Culturally and ethnically, Guangdong, which was inhabited by non-Chinese Miao and Yao peoples, was closer to the Gulf of Tongking. At the beginning of the Han dynasty, the kingdom constituted the kingdom of the Southern Yue and this name, Yuenan in Chinese, corresponds to the modern name of Vietnam. The military expeditions of the Qin First Emperor have only left the remnants of some garrisons and it was not until the end of the second century BC that an active policy of colonization undertaken by the Han Emperor Wudi began to confer a Chinese character on the region. This process was to last several centuries and, under the influence of the Chinese, coastal trade and exchanges with more distant regions   (south-east Asia, Taiwan, Indonesia) greatly expanded.

The Tomb
of the King
of the Southern Yue

The tomb of the King of the Southern Yue in the Western Han period, excavated in June 1983 at Xianggang, city of Guangzhou, is the largest tomb with a stone burial chamber in the Guangdong and Guangxi region. More than 1,000 objects have been found in the tomb, half of which are bronzes, such as this tripod in typical southern Yue style. Besides the garment of the king and numerous pi discs, the jade objects include the goblet illustrated below and the magnificent pierced pendant encrusted with gold illustrated opposite.

Of the 19 seals found in this tomb, the one above is one of the largest and bears the inscription "imperial seal of King Wen," revealing the occupant of the tomb to be the king of the second kingdom of the southern Yue.

YUNNAN

The relative scarcity of archaeological finds made in Guangdong contrasts with the wealth of objects that have been discovered since 1955 in the nearby province of Yunnan. There are historical reasons for this, since modern Yunnan enjoyed a prosperous independence from an early date, following the foundation of the Dian kingdom there at the end of the fourth century by a Chu general returning from an expedition. This kingdom then enjoyed some two centuries of peace, even escaping the expeditions of the Qin First Emperor and it was not until 109 BC that it became subject to the Han Emperor Wudi, who then awarded the Dian king a personal gold seal.

The richness of this mountain state was undoubtedly due to the peace it enjoyed but also the extent of its agriculture and the development of its trade. The region of Kunming, the modern capital of the province, was in fact a key area for communications with the peninsula of Indo-China and the fabrics and bamboo objects from Sichuan, further to the north, were carried through it. Archaeological finds show that the culture of the kingdom of Dian was a mixture of traditions brought by Chinese merchants and soldiers and indigenous or foreign ones. Animal art flowered to a quite exceptional degree and was imbued with all the vigour of the art of the steppes, and indeed certain burial customs are similar to those of north-west China.

A bronze model of a building. Inside there is a small niche, which contains the head of a man. The figures depicted are dancing or playing musical instruments — the scene is perhaps a family sacrifice.

Above: *The gold seal (length 2.4 cm. weight 90 g.) is incised with the characters "seal of the King of Dian." The ancient history, the Shiji, states that it was conferred as a mark of power by the Han court in the second year of the reign of Yuanfeng (109 BC).*

Left: *Bronze figurine of a kneeling maiden holding an umbrella (height 104 cm.).*

153

The art the kingdom of Dian is characterized by objects in which forms are fused, for example the drum, typical of the art of south east Asia, and a style which recalls motifs from the art of the steppes. The lid of this cowry container (the cowry shell was used as money) has 127 fused human figures celebrating a ceremony. The tribal chief is seated on the altar whilst animal sacrifices, dances and a banquet are proceeding around him. The handles are formed by two tigers and the feet are formed by the paws of animals.

Right: The lid of this cowry container (diameter 30 cm.) depicts a battle scene. It is the realistic and animated style of depiction which is the best feature of these artefacts.

154

Domestic and Wild Animals:
a Recurring Theme

Fights between animals and, still more often, an attack on a docile domestic animal by wild beasts or snakes is a recurrent theme in the art of the steppes from the first millennium BC onwards. On this bronze table (height 43 cm., weight 12.55 kg.) a buffalo is being attacked by a young tiger, with the calf beneath its belly providing a dramatic contrast.

Opposite: The bronze headrest (height 32.5 cm.) has a bas relief on its front of tigers tearing bulls apart.

In the ornamental plates, treated with a vigour which recalls that of full relief, the subject, except in the instance illustrated above of two dancers (very different from those of the Dian), is always a fight between animals. Below: A tiger leaps at the throat of a bull. Opposite: The strength of the imagery is even greater, as two wolves seize a fawn at the same time and convey with extraordinary immediacy the brutality of the scene.

EASTERN HAN DYNASTY

1ST - 2ND CENTURY A.D.

"The great town of the West sinks into chaos.
Ravaged by tigers and wolves,
Once again I am to be exiled from China
And live in servitude in Barbarian lands.
I have climbed the ridge of Baling to the South;
When I turn and look back at Chang'an,
I think of my dead, beside the Yellow Springs
And deep sighs rend my heart."

Above: *Three Han dignitaries. Cai Yong (133-192), an eminent intellectual ruler under the Eastern Hans, whose daughter was married to a barbarian king with whom she stayed for twelve years. Zhou Yafu, outstanding politician, in the service of emperors Wendi and Kingdi (from 179 to 139). Wei Qing, general of the Eastern Hans.*

The renewal of barbarian incursions into Chinese territory foreshadowed and at the same time precipitated the decline of the first Han. However, the underlying causes of the crisis did not lie in the insecurity of the frontiers but within the Empire. The power and solidity of the institutions had permitted the unprecedented economic growth of a great China. But this growth, by transforming the society and daily life, was at the root of the progressive decay of these very insitutions, ill adapted as thay were to the rise of a rich and powerful bourgeoisie.

The usurper Wang Man strove in vain with his Xin (Newness) dynasty from AD 9 to 23, but he failed to reverse the trend. Realizing the danger of increasing instability, the wealthy families helped to place a member of the imperial clan of the Liu on the throne. He took the name of Guang-wudi and moved the capital further east, to Luoyang; and thus began the period of the later or Eastern Han — their capital being situated further east than the earlier one of Chang'an. For a century, the former power and glory returned: prosperity within, tribute-paying countries beyond.

Classical studies, which had already been restored to a place of honour under the first Han witnessed an exceptional flowering. Works such as the "Classic of Poetry", the "Treatise on Music" (since lost), the rituals, the historical texts were again honoured, commented upon and put into practice. A strong Confucianist strand made itself felt at the same time as, more marginally, numerous esoteric philosophical or religious ideas were current in circles near the court. It is at this time, during the reign of the Emperor Mingdi (58-76) that the first notions of Buddhism are traditionally said to have arrived. All these movements of ideas were not unconnected with the intellectual ferment and the agitation which was gradually to take hold of the country and which paved the way for the decline of the central power. Little by little, the same internal conflicts that had overthrown the first Han dynasty grew. The situation was complicated by the appearance of messianic religious sects. Powerful and organized along the lines of a temporal power, they quickly posed a threat to the State, with their thousands of faithful, their meetings and their heterodox rites, their entry dues (five bushels of rice, for example) which evaded the State treasury. The high priests were sometimes more like chieftains, as in the movements of the Yellow Turbans or the Red Eyebrows. Power slipped from the Emperor and was regained by the great landed families and by the palace eunuchs; wandering soldiers or peasants administered the *coup de grace*. This was the beginning of a new era of divisions and local lords.

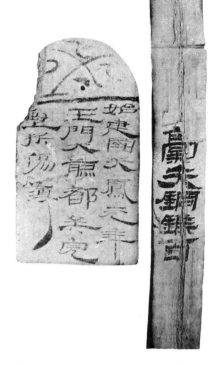

Fragments of paper and wooden tablets containing orders for missions, military reports and so on, found near the Great Wall.

SICHUAN

One can get a better idea of the original features of daily life in Yunnan from these scenes, which are bas-reliefs on funerary bricks preserved at Cheng-du, capital of Sichuan, rather than models in the round on the lids of jars. The scenes, both inside and outside the houses, are treated in a manner that it is both simple and vigorous and neither the buildings nor the garments display the exotic features of Yunnan. In artistic terms, the problems raised by perspective are tackled in an astonishingly novel way for the Eastern Han period, and the effect of depth is often skilfully rendered. The activites being performed are extremely varied and the actions of fishermen, hunters, workers in salt mines, reapers and household servants are perfectly depict-

ed. It is known that all this economic activity actually took place in the Sichuan of the Han: the lacquers were highly regarded and the casting of iron, the exploitation of salt mines, weaving and agricultural resources helped to build enormous fortunes. The peripheral position of Sichuan favoured this economic expansion, because the manufactured products enjoyed a natural, additional market in the countries of south-east Asia.

These funerary bricks recreate within the tomb a variety of scenes from daily life. Below: *The bustling activity of a granary.* Previous page: *A courtyard and a scene with musicians and dancers.*
On the following pages: *Centre, a procession, the entrance portal, a person seated in order to receive instructions and more scenes with musicians and dancers.*

163

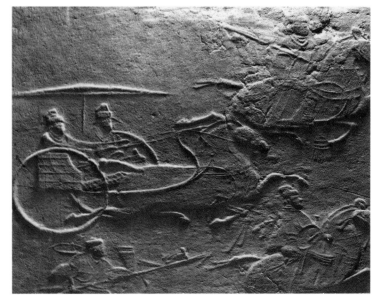

GANSU

Under the Han, Gansu saw intense military activity and an extensive programme of colonization. The generals of the Emperor Wudi engaged and thrust back the barbarian Xiongnu, established territories and built up defences. The later Han, despite the successes of General Ban Chao in Central Asia in the first century AD, were less aggressive; fortunately for them, the threat from the nomads of this region was also much less. It is unclear whether the policy the second Han continued and greatly strengthened in their dealings with the Xiongnu was dictated by weakness or strategy. The gifts made to the nomads of the steppes, and particularly to those of the oases of Central Asia multiplied to the point where at the end of the first century they were running to hundreds of millions of coins and millions of rolls of silk. Although this policy stimulated the crafts of China, raised the prestige of the Han and above all considerably developed the merchant economy of Gansu, and initiated the Silk Route its adverse effects were no less important, since it slowly but surely drained the public coffers and it ruined large numbers of Chinese farming families, many of whom had been settled by the Emperor Wudi in order to extend Chinese influence and establish the borders.

There are a considerable number of archaeological remains from this period in the oases and the caravan towns of northern Gansu, at Dunhuang, Wuwei, as far as Turfan

in the modern western province of Xinjiang and Juyan to the west of Inner Mongolia. The finds include evidence of Chinese administration, with large numbers of inscriptions on wooden slats or silk (certificates, military orders, legal declarations); wooden and iron farming implements; wooden figurines proud bronze horses and horsemen with their movements perfectly captured – typical examples of Han taste. These provide valuable information on the cultural mixture of the area. The superb bronze horses and horsemen, funerary figurines from the tomb of a Chinese general near Wuwei, reflect a profound understanding of horses and remind one that the cavalry was both the pride of the Han army and the only effective means of fighting the nomadic invaders, who were themselves bold horsemen

The four bronze figurines (height 22 cm.) bear on their backs the inscription "servants of Zhang."

Opposite: One of the most famous examples of Han sculpture, the galloping horse is captured in all the naturalness of its movement, with three hooves in the air and the fourth resting on a bird.

who appeared without warning and then disappeared back into the wild.

However, finished though their art is, these figurines should not make one forget the multitude of simply carved and painted wooden ones (draught oxen, real or mythical beasts) which testify to the skill of the local craftsmen.

Leitai,
the Tomb of a Han General

Top right: *The horse of the tomb's occupant stands out by its size (height 51 cm., length 41.5 cm.) and by its saddle and skirt.*

Above: *Two ladies in the service of Zhang and, right, a slave and a horse offered, as the inscription on the chest of the latter reads, by an official of low rank to the deceased "Governor of Zhangye."*

Opposite: *A horse which is stamping and neighing with unusual naturalism and expressive force (height 36.5-38 cm., length 34-36.5 cm.).*

In one of the side chambers of the tomb of Zhang bronze models of 14 different types of carriages, 39 horses, 17 soldiers and 28 servants have been found. Arranged in a procession, the two soldiers which lead it are of higher rank than those following, as can be seen from the ornament which surmounts their hats. The canopied shao carriage is reserved for the occupant of the tomb.

INNER MONGOLIA

Inner Mongolia, an autonomous administrative region, lies to the south of Outer Mongolia, a member of the Soviet bloc, which covers three times its area but has only a fifth of the population. The majority of Inner Mongolia's 6.5 million inhabitants live near the borders of the neighbouring provinces of Shenxi, Shanxi and Hebei. It would be too simplistic to view Mongolia, a land beyond the Great Wall peopled by nomadic horsemen who tended herds and hunted, as a homogenous state under the Han and thereafter which was radically different from the adjacent Chinese provinces. Although Mongol power finally, in the thirteenth century, placed the first foreign dynasty, the Yuan, on the throne of an undivided China, the Mongol threat was no greater at other periods than that posed by the Xiongnu and the Jurchen. The Great Wall, by defining a border zone where at times a trade flourished in horses and Chinese products, helped to bring together the civilizations of the steppes and China as much as it kept them apart.

Under the later Han, the inhabitants of modern Mongolia benefitted from the policy of the Chinese towards the Barbarians, which was the same as the one they pursued towards the Xiongnu in Gansu. They received presents, particularly silks, in exchange for peace and their support for the Empire. In fact, many nomad horsemen joined the Han armies and in the course of the first two centuries the peasant families who were moved to Mongolia and the Chinese officials who were posted there partly succeeded in getting the nomadic populations to settle down.

This process has left numerous archaeological traces. As in Gansu, there are administrative texts written on wooden strips or even wall paintings, such as those of the Helinger tombs, near Huheot, which portray festive scenes, tilling, processions of chariots and the interiors of houses. The artistry is far from being as complete as, for example, that of the funerary bricks of Sichuan and it resembles that of the painted bricks dating from the third century AD discovered at Jiayuguan in Gansu. Undoubtedly, artistic expression was somewhat crude at that period, particularly on the northern borders of China. Be that as it may, the themes are entirely Chinese and there is nothing surprising about this when one remembers that Helinger was only a hundred kilometres away from the great town of Datong in northern Shanxi.

The nomads, by virtue of their way of life, tended to use perishable materials, which have in many cases not survived down to the present day. However, the array of jewels with animal motifs, sometimes in gold and semiprecious stones, which have been discovered at various sites in modern Inner Mongolia, are purely local artefacts which leave no room for doubt about the skill and ability of the craftsmen of the steppes.

The Horinger Tombs
and their Wall Paintings

In Inner Mongolia, a land of horse breeding, there are numerous Han tombs with wall paintings of themes connected with horses, and also astronomical motifs.

Opposite: The departure of a carriage, horses chasing each other and horses drawn up on parade.

A Procession
in Sha'anxi

The Han tomb excavated at Yangjia-wan, in the city of Xianyang, contained a terracotta army several strong

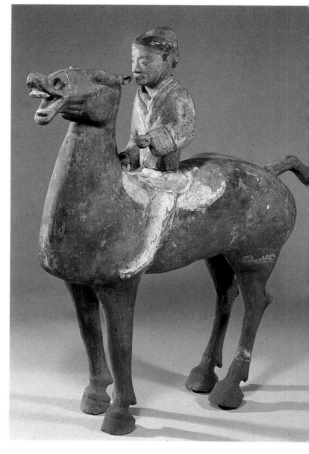

(height 48-48.5 cm.) arranged in order of battle. The formation is led by musicians whose instruments — probably made of wood — have disappeared. The eight horsemen, like other statuettes found in the same region, ride mounts whose vigour is quite beyond that of the docile horses of the guard of the First Emperor. One theory is that these horses are a new breed of mixed blood descended from the horse of Bactria, very different from the pony of ancient China.

FOUR CENTURIES OF STRUGGLE

THE CHINESE MIDDLE AGES

Beginning in the third century in China there was a further intermingling of different populations, with the Han being the principal element. In the Wei and Jin period and during the subsequent one of the Northern and Southern Dynasties, the central plains were subject to constant warfare, whilst along the middle and lower valley of the Changjiang there was a considerable economic expansion as a result of many years of effort by the kingdom of Wu. The divided China of this period constitutes a link between the past and future – a preliminary for the economic and cultural flowering of the Tang dynasty.

With the decline of the Xiongnu and the rise of the Xianbei, the Toba founded the dynasty of the Northern Wei (AD 386-534) in northern China. The grave goods found in a tomb excavated in the village of Meidai in the autonomous region of Inner Mongolia are a typical feature of Xianbei culture in its initial phase. The various finds include a bronze axe and a Xiongnu style belt buckle indicate that at the start of their reign the Toba absorbed numerous characteristics of the preceding culture, a *pan* with a handle in the form of a dragon's head reveals the influence of Han culture whilst the goat astragal is typical of nomadic populations. Towards the end of the era of the Northern Wei, the grave goods cease to be distinguishable from those of the central plains – a phenomenon which shows the assimilation of Han culture by the Wei.

The tomb of Feng Sufu, a member of the royal family of the Northern Yan, was discovered at Beipiao in Liaoning in 1965. It revealed that the northern populations continued to intermingle during the period of the 16 Kingdoms (beginning of the fourth century). The finds reveal a strong local character and they illustrate the habits and traditions of the Xianbei, revealing at the same time the similarities with the grave goods of the Han upper classes. Wall paintings, for example, depict such themes as maps of the heavens, processions and scenes from family life.

The tombs of this period testify to the rise of rich and powerful families at the end of the Eastern Han dynasty. A large number of family burial grounds have been found both in the north and south in which epitaphs giving the history of the family, the life and the social status of the occupants begin to appear. In some cases land titles, on which are recorded the areas and values of the lands bought by the deceased are also preserved in the tombs.

The most important finds include the coloured wooden screens with lacquer pictures which have been uncovered in the Northern Wei tomb of Sima Jinglong (AD 484) in the city of Datong, in Shanxi. The subjects of the paintings are emperors, generals, ministers, virtuous ladies and obedient sons, accompanied by numerous poems and explanatory texts which consitute an unusual detail. The tombs of this period have also yielded fine, elegant porcelains.

The district of Cixian, Hebei, on the north-western edge of the capital of Yecheng, contains the burial place of the

Detail of a lacquered wooden panel from the tomb of Sima Jinglong at Datong, Shanxi.

noble and royal families of the Eastern Wei and the Northern Qi periods. The second capital of the Northern Qi dynasty was Taiyuan, where tombs of Eastern Wei and Northern Qi families have recently been excavated. The finds include wall paintings, terracotta and porcelain figurines. Recently tombs of the Northern Dynasties have been discovered, in particular that of Lou Rui, an influential and well known figure, who was related to an empress. The corridors and chambers of his tomb were covered by 200 square metres of wall paintings. There were more than 800 burial objects, including 600 terracotta figurines. The discovery of these pictures, which had been mentioned in historical documents, filled some gaps in the history of Chinese art.

The Six Dynasties (AD 220-539) which followed had as their capital the modern city of Nanjing in Jiangsu (which bore the name of Jianye at the time of the Eastern Wu and Jiankang at a later date). Naturally, as a capital it was both

Stone statues guarding the entrances to the tombs of high ranking persons have been found at more than three hundred sites in Nanjing and the district of Danyang. Here two lions and a pair of "pillars of the road of the spirits" defend the Xiao Ji tomb of the Prince Nankangjian, who died in the third year of the reign of Datong (AD 529) of the Liang dynasty.

the economic and cultural centre, and the royal tombs of several dynasties are situated in its vicinity. On the basis of literary sources, 71 such tombs have been found here and in the districts of Danyang, Jiangling and Jurong and 31 of them have remains protruding above ground level. Eight royal tombs have been excavated, three of which were without visible trace.

It was at this time that the custom of burying all the members of a clan in a single burial ground became prevalent. The emperors of the Qi and Liang dynasties all came from Danyang and were therefore buried here. The entrances to their tombs were guarded by large statues. Excavations have been carried out in the burial grounds of various great families: the six tombs of the Zhou family at Yixing, which occupy an area of 57,000 square metres, and the seven tombs of the Wang family at Xianshan near Najing, which cover an overall area of 50,000 square metres.

During this period the tombs were situated on the side or at the base of a hill, a rectangular cavity was prepared and inside this a walled chamber was built; with this arrangement a burial shaft was unnecessary.

The majority of tombs had a single chamber with walls

of bricks bearing reliefs and one or two arched doorways with reliefs on their pediments. The chambers usually had a drainage system in order to allow water to flow out, a new feature which occurs only rarely in the tombs of other periods in southern China and those of the semi-arid lands of northern China. Buildings intended for ceremonial purposes, which once surmounted the tombs, have collapsed and the remains of carved stones are scattered in the vicinity. With the advent of the People's Republic work began restoring these carved stones, which are derived from the Han tradition, uniting local and imported motifs to form a unique and unusual style. The decoration of the walls with incised bricks is another instance of the persistence of specific Han motifs. The theme of the mythical monster is Han in origin and the use of moulds in manufacturing the brick to achieve high reliefs is likewise traditional. Scenes on individual bricks were replaced by large mosaics and the themes included the traditional white tigers and blue dragons, guardian lions and soldiers armed with lances, as well as horsemen. One picture in particular deserves a mention, *The Seven Sages of the Bamboo Thicket* perfectly reflects the spirit of the scholars of the time — original, decadent, each with a marked personality and separated by various types of plants in which the artist reveals his imagination.

Celadon reached new heights in the techniques of firing and manufacture. Scientific examination of the objects discovered in the kilns of Yixing and Nanjing show that the firing was carried out at temperatures between 1160 and 1260 degrees centigrade with an absorption of 3-7 per cent.

These objects are markedly harder and have much purer glazes than the glazed pottery of the Han dynasty. The commonest forms in the period of the Eastern Wu are the *bo* cup, the *guan* two-handled jug, the *yu* bowl, oil lamps and models which served as grave goods, such as granaries, kilns, hen-houses and so on. During the Jin dynasty a wide variety of new forms appeared and at the same time the forms of the artefacts acquired a zoomorphic decoration: the mouths and spouts of vessels took the form of chickens' or tigers' heads, whilst the handles became dragons. At the end of the period of the Six Dynasties, the constant use of the lotus on celadon reflected the spread of Buddhism.

NORTHERN AND SOUTHERN DYNASTIES

3RD - 6TH CENTURY A.D.

The Northern Wei, who were of barbarian origin, became one of the most powerful dynasties during this turbulent period. Here the Emperor Taiwu-di (424-451) is on the throne, surrounded by his ministers, each of whom holds a jade tablet in his hand, a symbol of his office.

The history of China after the final and official collapse of the Han in AD 220 is like a novel where the mighty of one day are defeated the next, where the claimants to a local lordship might be rich Chinese squires or barbarian tribes, the latter regularly driving out the former in the provinces of the lower Yangzi. The chapters of this novel bear such fabulous titles as the Three Kingdoms, the Six Kingdoms of the Five Barbarians, the Six Dynasties. These centuries, which tried and matured the institutions of China, were full of changes of fortune and colourful characters (warriors and strategists).

Put very simply, power in Northern China at this time, above all in the Yellow River basin, was lost by Chinese squires on several occasions from the beginning of the fourth century onwards and passed to barbarians, who quickly became assimilated. Although the South was not peaceful, it did enjoy an economic prosperity that had several profound consequences. To begin with it gradually eliminated the aristocrats, whether local or from the North, from the highest political level, to the benefit of a flourishing mercantile bourgeoisie. Above all, it gave the South an historical importance which until then the provinces of the North had often monopolized and which it would never give up. It was this period, for example, that saw the growth of Nanking, which was to be the capital of the dynasties of the South for two and a half centuries. The settled nomads which followed each other at Luoyang and Chang'an, these two cities generally continuing to be the capitals, having rapidly adopted a strong, legalist form of government into which they breathed a new vigour, and Chinese institutions, far from emerging weakened, seemed to come out of these troubled centuries with a certificate of viability conferred by the ancient barbarians of the steppe.

The wars of expansion of the new northern rulers towards the lower Yangzi were not conducted in any systematic fashion. The South was prosperous and of a size to defend itself. In addition the Northern Kingdoms had their hands full in dealing with the incursions of the Ruan-ruan, the Xia and other barbarians. Greater benefits could often be obtained from trade. Steel, brocades, ceramics and luxury products were greatly appreciated in the North, and the Emperor Xiaowen of the Northern Wei would even, as an act of admiration at the beginning of the sixth century, rebuild his capital of Luoyang, which had 500,000 inhabitants, on the model of Nanking, with more than a million.

This period has been called the Chinese Middle Ages but whereas in Europe the Renaissance followed the Middle Ages in China the equivalent phenomena coexisted at the same time. On the one hand there was a development of religious fervour in all classes of society whilst on the other there was the extraordinary refinement towards which art of the scholars evolved in poetry and music, in calligraphy and painting. The scholars, officials who had survived from extinct dynasties or victims of unjust treatment, often

The Emperor Wendi, the first of the Wei, one of the Three Kingdoms which succeeded the Han and which dominated China in the third century.

Ma Lin: "Listening to Wind amongst the Pines", painted on silk, dated 1246.

"I reside therefore on my
own, governing my vital
energy;
I prepare my cup to drink, I
play my cithara;
I unroll paintings and view
them in seclusion, exploring
the regions of the world
while remaining seated.
Without running away from
all my misfortunes, my
solitude echoes the wild
emptiness of nature.
The peaks and summits
tower grandly, the thick
forests in the distance are
swathed in cloud; the
brilliance of the saints and
the sages shall never fade,
and all phenomena are
resplendent with their
genius. . ."

sought in the literary circles of initiates or in their seclusion in the countryside a means of escaping from the vicissitudes of the world. It was at this time that the poet Tao Yuan-ming (365-427) wrote his poem "Return to Country Life":

"As a young man without inclination for the rat race,
With innate good taste, I loved the mountains.
Fallen inadvertently into the snare of time
For a stretch, it cost me thirteen years!
The caged bird dreams of its ancestral wood,

The fish in the bowl of its native stream.
Clearing my land in the wastes of the South,
Still a rustic at heart I have returned to the land
Nothing reaches my home of the hurly burly;
In my isolated resting place, I have my fill of leisure.
I long lived as in a cage;
Here I have finally returned to myself."

Such returns to the sources of nature did, sometimes, lead to a certain disenchantment. However, scholars were not alone in no longer believing in the values of this world, and the renunciation by some strata of society was also expressed in the adoption of the values of a rather specific Chinese Buddhism. The taking of vows also brought a relative degree of physical and material security. On a number of occasions, under the direction of particularly devout rulers, the Buddhist clergy became a major moral and economic force within the State. The number of monasteries in the lower Yangzi reached 13,000 at the beginning of the sixth century. The expenditure on luxuries occasioned by the casting of statues, as well as the size of the gifts and the extent of the privileges enjoyed by the monks were such that the economy was often strained. Then in 446, 470 and 574, for instance, mass persecution and forced secularisation took place. In the meantime Buddhism grew considerably and pilgrimages transformed the life of entire regions, such as the oases of Gansu, which formed the Silk Route but also the road to India. The first caves of Dunhuang began to be frescoed at the end of the fourth century and a century later monumental Buddhist statues were begun at two particularly impressive sites, one at Yungang near Datong and the other at Longmen near Luoyang: the Buddhas carved out of the stone cliffs were more than 40 metres high.

Buddhist pilgrim in a ninth century painting from Dunhuang.

189

Princess Ru Ru and her Escort

In 1979 the tomb of a young princess was discovered in the district of Ci-xian, Hebei. She was a member of an

ethnic minority in northern China and the wife of the son of Gao Huan. Gao Huan exercised undisputed power under the Western Wei and finally supplanted the Wei Emperor and founded the dynasty of the Northern Qi.

In the tomb of the princess, who died at the tender age of 13, more than 1,000 terracotta figurines have been found, including the "Sa Man" (above), a shaman of this ethnic minority, who dances in a trance with a musical instrument in his hand. As always, the variety of the figures is extraordinary.

191

Warriors, Officials, Ladies of the Court

Right: *A lady of the court, distinguished by a long red tunic, and a terracotta figurine of a warrior with a shield (height 43-48 cm.). The martial expression on his face and his stiff posture convey his function as a guard.*

Opposite, below: *Palace maidens (height 18.5-20 cm.) dressed in flowing garments with wide sleeves with their hair wound on top of their heads or gathered at the side.*

Top: *A group of kneeling figures (a total of 46 figurines) awaiting an audience.*

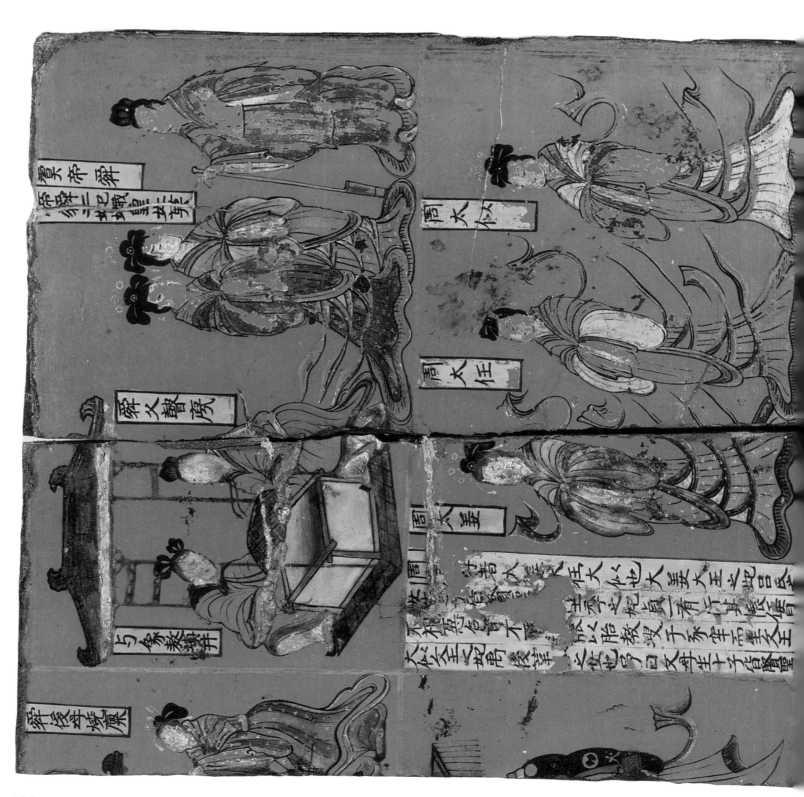

These painted wooden panels have been unearthed from the tomb of Sima Jinlong, who died in 484 and whose tomb was excavated from 1966 onwards. Jinlong (dragon of gold) belonged to the ancient imperial clan of the Sima and it is quite in keeping for his tomb to have been richly decorated (terracotta figurines, wooden carvings and so on). These five wooden panels illustrate the exemplary life of various virtuous persons made famous by the hagiographic collections: virtuous wives and concubines, pious sons and upright ministers from remote antiquity to the Han are shown performing their great works according to the Confucian ideal.

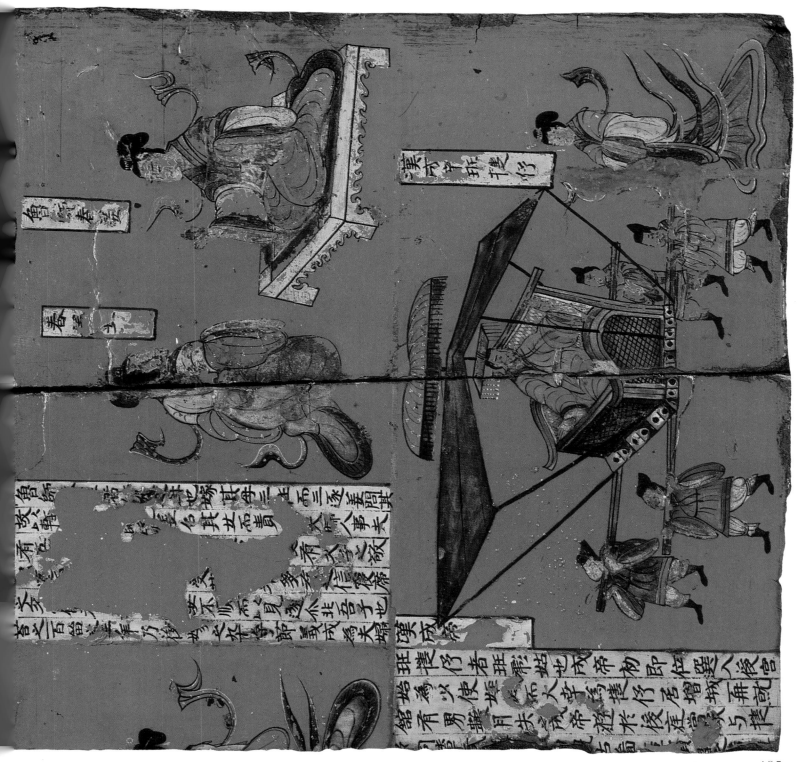

SHANXI

Shanxi was the seat, from the end of the fourth century to the end of the fifth, of the first capital of one of the most powerful of the northern dynasties, which was near Datong, in the north of the province, close to the Great Wall. It was here that the barbarian Toba founded their Wei dynasty (386-534), which was associated with an as then unprecedented flowering of Buddhism and its art. At that time the route from Central Asia was still open, allowing the religions movement from India, and the numbers of translations of Indian works, tales of pilgrimage and philosophical cum religious works increased day by day and the monasteries became wealthier and wealthier. The temporal power of the monks was at times fabulous and the religious authority of some of them was such that the leader of a Buddhist community in the Yangzi valley, Huiyuan (334-417), simply decreed one day that Buddhist monks *shamen* did not have to salute the person of the emperor. At another time, this crime of *lèse-majesté* would not have gone unpunished.

Apart from the Buddhist statuary, which overshadows other artistic endeavours, the Shanxi of this period is better known today through the recent discovery of several tombs of important figures dating from the end of the fifth and the early sixth century, where one can see members of the Chinese gentry in the wall paintings. One of the tombs is the mausoleum of a member of the famous Sima clan at Datong, the capital.

The entrance to the tomb of Lou Rui on the edge of Taiyuan, Shanxi. The tomb is decorated with wall paintings that cover a total of 200 square

metres. More than 800 funerary objects have been found inside the tomb, including celadon and porcelain items with appliqued decoration. These include the lamp and the vase illustrated here, which are rare examples of decoration derived from the forms of gold and silver objects.

The entrance portal, with five carved lotus flowers and interlaced branches.

Lou Rui,
Extravagant and Profligate Courtier

The only example of wall painting under the Northern Qi, the paintings depict in vivid colours and with a delicacy of treatment which distinguishes the art of the Han, the life of this influential figure, a member of the imperial family. Below: A banquet in honour of a foreign dignitary and, opposite, a guard of honour.

On the upper part of the funerary chamber is the legendary residence of the soul after death. The ox is one of the twelve symbols of the astrological calendar, a representation of the "twelve earthly branches" which indicate the year of a person's birth.

Below and on the following page: The funerary procession on the west wall of the tomb's passageway. Opposite: A chariot drawn by oxen.

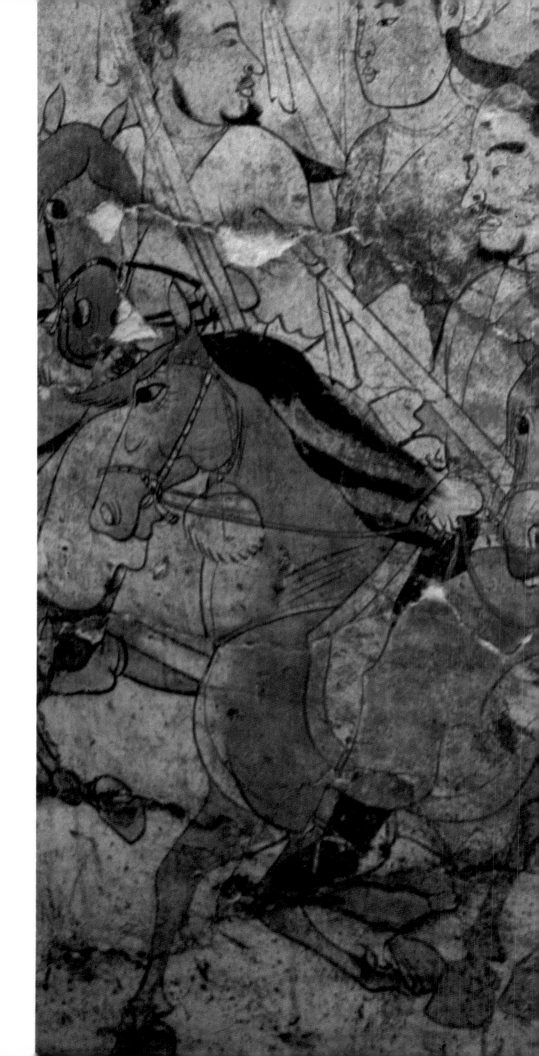

JIANGSU

Nanking and its province, Jiangsu, constituted the other pole in the history of the dynasties of the South. It was the seat of four dynasties in succession: the Song, the Qin, the Liang and the Chen. An eventful, sometimes troubled history, where *coups d'état* might be carried out in accordance with rites and customs and with all necessary humanity. This was the way that the first and the only real Liang emperor (his four successors only ruled for a year apiece) rose to power in 502, after he had already turned down the throne on several occasions despite having done everything to attain it. On his accession he assumed the illustrious name of the Emperor Wudi.

It was under him that Jiangsu enjoyed its golden age, although the Wei always threatened in the North, despite the fruitful commercial links which developed with them. Then, in 557, a part of the barbarian aristocracy that had been established in the north-west, the Western Wei, rejecting all attempts at sinification, moved to overthrow the dynasty. However, trade and the attractions of wealth made them forget their threats and a merchant class expanded greatly, at the same time as the market towns of the lower Yangzi were opened to foreign merchants, to trade of all kinds and to a hinterland which stretched back to Sichuan. This early commercial flowering of southern China was short-lived but the wealth that resulted can be seen in the few archaeological sites which have so far been explored.

The tombs have yielded
numerous proto-celadons of
animals or with zoomorphic
motifs, as well as Buddhist
bronze statues whose style
is radically different from
those of the north.
The powerful men of Jiangsu
also valued stone statuary,
particularly non-Buddhist ones,
unlike the barbarians of the
north, who prized the more or
less successful carving of entire
cliffs in the form of the Buddha.
Numerous tombs of noble or
princely families also has surface
decorations of chimeras and
lions, whose treatment was
always interesting and sometimes
successful. The heavy majesty of
these animals somewhat recalls
that of Han statuary but there is
always a certain mannerism.

Fabulous beasts exclusively set up in propitiation and as a symbol of authority on imperial tombs. The main difference between them is in the number of horns on the head. The qilin, *to the left (length 3.19 m., height 3.15 m.) is a unicorn which stands before the Yongning tomb of Chen Qianm Emperor Weni of the Chen dynasty at Ganjiaxiang, Nanjing, whereas the tinlu (length 3.15 m., height 2.80 m.), top right, which defends the tomb of the Emperor Wu of the Liang dynasty at Quia'aimaio Danang, has two horns.*

Clothed Bears, Bizarre Monsters:
The Celadons of the Eastern Jin

A variety of vases from several tombs dating from the Eastern Jin period have returned to the technique of incised decoration beneath the glaze, in conjunction with appliqued motifs.

A zun vase (height 20.3 cm., length 26 cm.) in the form of a ram with a brilliant blue glaze excavated from an Eastern Jin tomb at Xigang, Nanjing.

Left: *Celadon incense burner (height 19 cm., diameter of the globe 12.1 cm.) found in an Eastern Jin tomb dating from the seventh year of the reign of Yuankuang (AD 297) at Yixing.*

Below: *Celadon lamp supported by a clothed bear. It is marked on its base with the year in which it was made — the first year of the reign of Ganlu (AD 265).*

THE FLOWERING OF THE ARTS

SUI AND TANG DYNASTIES

Typical example of Tang art; terracotta with three-coloured glaze, sancai.

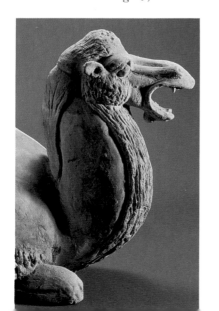

In the course of the Sui and Tang dynasties China experienced the greatest flowering of its arts. From 1957 onwards archaeologists concentrated their work on the excavations of the site of Chang'an, the capital which, in the seventh century, was one of the largest and most prosperous in the world, with a regular grid of streets, closed alleys and rigorously controlled markets, making it completely different from a European city.

The city of Chang'an enfolds the city of the palace, the imperial city and the outer city. The first of these lies north of the central part, whilst to the south, separated by a 220 metre avenue, stretches the imperial city, the administrative centre. The outer walls of the city were made of compressed earth and surrounded and protected the palace and imperial cities to the east, south and west. The foundations of the walls have only partly disappeared and are now, for the most part, at a depth of 0.5-1.5 metres, and at some points rise to three metres above the ground. The walls of the city measure 9,721 metres from east to west and 8,651 metres from north to south. The avenue of the Gate of the Red Bird forms the central axis of the city and 11 roads divide the city from north to south and 14 from east to west, with the result that the residential areas were divided into 109 blocks. To the east and west, the Dongshi and Xinshi markets were traversed by four avenues and formed the lively commercial districts of the capital, with numerous shops. The residential area reserved for the Tang emperors comprised three groups of palaces: the Taiji palace in the imperial city, the Daming palace and the Longshonyan palace to the north east of the city (built in 634) and the Xingqing palace in the south-east.

In October 1970, two urns containing finds, the most important of which were more than 1000 gold and silver objects amassed during the Tang dynasty, were uncovered in the village of Hejia on the southern edge of Xian. The site of the excavations was the residence of Prince Feng in Xinghua avenue, on the southern side of the south-east corner of the Tang imperial city. The gold and silver objects brought to light were highly elaborate, exquisitely made and displaying a high degree of craftsmanship, with decorative motifs distinguished by rich and vivid colours.

The tombs of the Tang emperors are situated in 18 localities scattered over six districts around Xi'an, usually at the foot of a hill. The tombs are modelled on the plan of Chang'an and each has a double gate. In front of the tomb there were stone sculptures: lions symbolizing the guardians, horses and riders forming the guard of honour, winged horses and foreign figures and ostriches, which indicate the contacts of China with the outside world, stone columns marking the site of the tomb and stone tablets. Near the tomb of the emperor there were satellite tombs for the members of his family and his favourite ministers and generals. The tomb of the Emperor Tai Zong is surrounded by 167 such tombs.

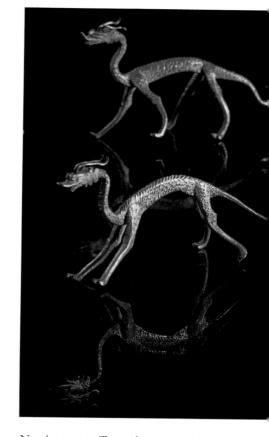

Nearly 2,000 Tang dynasty tombs have been discovered near Chang'an, the capital of the empire and one of the largest cities of its period. Numerous gold and silver artefacts have been found, including these dragon figurines made of gold thread.

Large groups of Sui and Tang tombs are also found on the edge of Chang'an. The tomb of Li Jingxun, excavated near the village of Liangjia, to the west of Xian, in 1957, is that of a nine year old girl buried in the fourth year of the reign of Daye of the Sui dynasty (AD 608). She was related to the imperial family and this explains the abundance of grave goods. The sarcophagus is exquisitely made, the lid of the coffin takes the form of a roof with nine sloping surfaces, and there are engraved doors, windows, pilasters and

Polychrome Tang ceramics, which were achieved by using metal oxides, display a rich range of coloured glazes, including yellow, green, brown, blue and white.

flower motifs. The finds include a highly important necklace of granulated gold set with 28 precious stones. Three tombs of the Du Gu Si Zhen family were excavated in the village of Hong Qing on the north-eastern edge and the tomb of Xian Yu Jing Hui in the village of Nanhe on the eastern edge have all yielded elegant three-coloured Tang figurines (*san cai*), which are highly realistic and vividly coloured — a reflection of the highly developed techniques employed in Tang ceramics. The tombs of Li Zhongzun (682-701), hereditary prince of Yide and Li Xian (654-684), hereditary prince of Zhangwai were excavated in the district of Qian Xian, Sha'anxi province in July 1971. Both had long access ramps, skylights, passages, arches, front and rear chambers. Apart from Xian, investigations and explorative excavations have also been carried out in the Tang capital of Luoyang and here too a plethora of elegant, three-coloured ceramics has been unearthed. Luoyang, the second capital of the Tang dynasty, lay in the central plains and occupied a key position for Chang'an, linking the zone of Guandong with the south east. Ceramics were widely produced here by craftsmen but differed from the ceramics of Xi'an in the richness of their decoration, those of Xi'an being simple and delicate while Luonyang motifs were more sumptuous and varied. The subjects depicted also reflect the trading activity of the Chinese and the merchants of western Asia along the Silk Route.

More than 2,000 Sui and Tang tombs have been excavated in the neighbourhood of the ancient site of Chang'an and some 200 of these are datable or bear epitaphs. Research carried out on this group of tombs has shown that under the Sui at the beginning of the Tang period the tombs tended to have long, sloping passages, numerous air inlets and small sanctuaries, reproducing, to some extent, the dwellings of the living. Funerary figurines – chariots, initially drawn by oxen, then by camels and horses – and wall paintings, mainly depicting processions, were the commonest features. Mid-way through the Tang period the corridors were shortened and the number of air intakes and shrines were reduced, but great attention was lavished on the structure of the burial chamber. The fashion at this time was to prepare sets of grave goods comprising three-coloured ceramic models of rocks and buildings, with the emphasis on the depiction of daily life rather than on processions. Towards the end of the Tang the building of costly tombs with gold and silver ornament and embroidered grave goods became common practice. These objects were predominantly bronze mirrors and ceramic artefacts. The techniques for the manufacture of mirrors show a marked advance around the middle of the Tang. As well as round and square mirrors, octagonal, lozenge and sunflower-shaped ones appeared, plated with gold or silver or encrusted with mother-of-pearl or turquoise. Other examples were burnished with gold or silver inlays and embossed decoration.

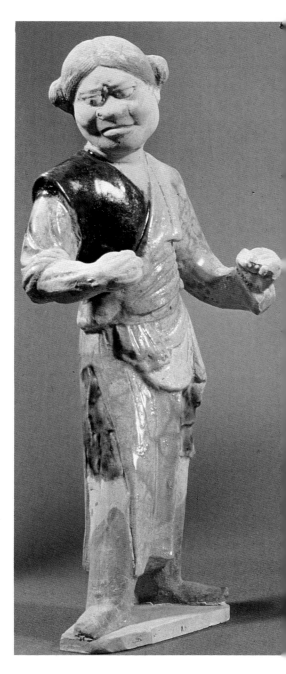

Three-coloured ceramic groom (height 28.5 cm.). Highly expressive, and carefully executed with a lively face, he holds a horse by the bridle, a recurring subject in the grave goods of the Tang dynasty.

In 1970, two jars were uncovered in a Tang cellar in the village of Hejia (once the Xinhua avenue of the city of Chang'an) on the southern edge of Xi'an. Amongst the 1,000 objects it contained there were 270 gold or silver ones, which had never before been found in such numbers or displaying such exquisite workmanship. The finds included an agate cup with an animal head and gold inlay, a Byzantine gold coin bearing the profile of Heraclius (610-641), a Sasanian silver coin of King Chosroes II (590-627) and five Wakokaichin silver coins from Japan (708-715), which provide evidence of the exchanges between China and other countries during the Tang dynasty.

The majority of Tang tombs discovered in other areas are similar to those found near Chang'an, but some do display distinctive features: at Astana, in the village of Karallja in the autonomous region of Xingjiang Uygur, a large number of documents, silk paintings and other artefacts have been found. In the passageway of the tomb of the Princess Zhenhai in the burial ground of the principality of Bohai (in the modern district of Dunhua, Jieling) a pair of stone lions of Tang manufacture has been found, similarly, the Chinese epitaph which describes the princess is an exact copy of a Tang epitaph. The upper part of the tomb, however, displays similarities with the Kokuli tombstones typical of the region. It provides therefore evidence of both the influx of the Kokuli tradition and the profound penetration of Tang culture.

Above: Hunter on horseback with a dog. The colours are obtained by mixing the glazes with the clay, using a special firing technique, the "Jiao Tai"; this is one of the few surviving examples. Opposite: A particularly good three-coloured ceramic statuette of a seated lady (height 33.8 cm.). The features of the face are painted and the eyebrows are finely drawn. She is wearing a blouse with tight sleeves and a pleated skirt. Over her shoulders she has a shawl and in her right hand, level with her chest, she holds a bunch of flowers.

SUI AND TANG DYNASTIES

581 - 618
618 - 917

In 581 a general from an aristocratic Northern family founded a new dynasty, the Sui. This dynasty could have been like the previous ones both in its internal policy and in its general place within a China that was still divided. This was not the case because things had changed in China as a result of the slow fermentation of the four preceding centuries. The rivalry between the various states, the contributions from Central Asia and the steppes with the regenerative influence of the nomads, the perspectives offered by the expansion of country to the maritime zones of Southern China and South-East Asia, the social, economic and cultural consequences of the general establishment of Buddhism: all this had moulded a new combination.

In much the same way as the First Emperor, Qin Shi Huangdi, had benefitted in unifying China at the end of the third century BC from the mixing and contact between regions during the preceding Warring States period, the emperor of the new dynasty, Wendi of the Sui, the "Scholar Emperor", benefitted from the numerous exchanges which had gradually developed between the Northern and South-

Top: *Polychrome statue of a divinity in the sanctuary at the entrance to cave 45 at Mogao, near Dunhuang, Gansu province; evidence of the stylistic heights attained by Buddhist iconography in China.*

ern dynasties. There was therefore nothing surprising in the fact that shortly after his coming to power he managed to reunite the whole country and to restore it to roughly the same size as it had had under the Han. Yangdi, his son and successor to the throne, who moreover had him assassinated, even planned the domination of Korea, as in the time of the Han Emperor Wudi. However, he had overextended himself and his disasterous expedition to the peninsula led to his downfall. One could again draw a parallel with the tyrant of the Qin, since there would be more than five million poor wretches – including women and children – that Yangdi mobilized to restore the Great Wall and extend it in the North West, to improve the road network, to rebuild the capital and the palace on a magnificent scale and, above all, to dig the Grand Canal in record time in about 608, linking the Peking region to the mouth of the Yangzi. It is said that half of them died, which, given that China then had a population of about 55 million, emptied a large number of prisons and left many villages abandoned.

This treatment, accompanied by an agrarian reform which was probably too major to be applied all at once, ended by exhausting the country. Following a traditional scenario, a general of the Li clan profited from the discontent of the peasants, to seize Chang'an. Overthrowing the Sui, he founded the Tang dynasty in 618 while Yangdi was executed at Yangzhou. The new emperor, Gaozu, the "Great Ancestor", had the benefit of a solid administrative system, which he improved still further by introducing fiscal laws, new agrarian regulations and a legal code. This code, promulgated for the first time in 627, had a decisive influence on the formation of Japanese laws.

On the political side, there was no break between the Sui and Tang dynasties, nor is there any clearer distinction in their art, particularly as the short duration of the Sui did not permit a distinctive style to blossom. It is only amongst some of the terracotta figurines that have been discovered that it is possible to draw a distinction by the style of the

Although Li Shi-min was not the first official emperor of the great Tang dynasty he was nevertheless its true founder. Known as the Taizong Emperor (626-49), he reorganized the army, particularly the cavalry, and he encouraged a major development of the economy and international exchange.

217

garments and perhaps also by a certain plastic coarseness. However, the major strands of Tang art were already apparent, strands which will continue until the tenth century: a realism that breaks with the pronounced taste for the supernatural of the preceding periods, cosmopolitan influences reflecting the manifold contacts with foreign civilizations (Arab, Turkish, Indian, etc.), finally the vigour of a dynasty which achieved peace on its frontiers by great feats of arms and glory beyond.

When he died in 649, the Emperor Taizong, the son of the founder of the Tang, had established Chinese domination as far as Turkestan, along the length of the Silk Route. His army and generals were excellent and, above all, he had a cavalry the like of which had not been seen since the Han. Naturally, the iconography of the Tang period is rich in military, equestrian and barbarian themes. However, as in previous epochs, much of the artists' work was devoted to Buddhist pieces and it is therefore also in the religious statues, frescos and other paintings that the splendour of the period is apparent. Finally, letters, particularly poetry, also flourished and China has perhaps never known greater poets than those of the Tang. Many of these poets were or had been officials recruited by means of examinations, a great innovation of the period, and sometimes also belonged to the Imperial Academy or the Imperial Conservatory, the "Pear-Tree Garden". Both of these were founded by the man who was to lead the dynasty to its apogee and who also caused its decline: the Emperor Xuanzong, who reigned from 713 to 756.

The emperor, lost in contemplation, did not see that affairs of state were pressing, that the barbarians were again at the frontiers, that a cousin of his concubine, named An Lushan, was seizing power. He had to flee, to allow, in despair, the beautiful concubine Guifei to be executed by his own soldiers, and it took eight years of reconquest before the poet Du Fu could write:

"Unexpected news at Jian'an: Jizhou retaken!

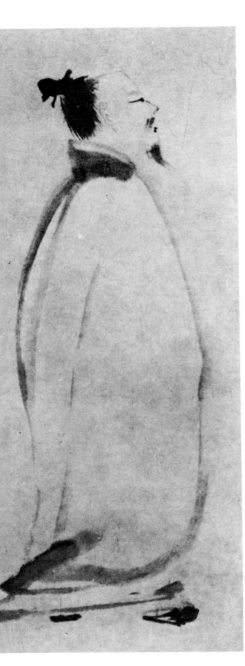

Li Bo reciting a poem.
The great Tang poet, known for his passion for wine, as well as his verses, is said to have drowned whilst leaning out from his boat to kiss the moon's reflection on the surface of the river.

Tears of joy drench my clothes.
I turn to my wife and my children:
where are you, sadness?
I roll up my books, haphazardly,
beside myself with joy. . ."

However, the return to Luoyang and the re-establishment of the dynasty was not the starting point of a new flowering. Later on in the same century, fifty years after the regency of the Empress Wu, another former imperial concubine, a lady of the palace, precipitated the decline. The Tang emperors who followed until the fall of the dynasty could not prevent the loss of Central Asia, the Tibetan invasion and the occupation of the Gansu oases, the ruin of the well-developed irrigation system which had ensured the richness of the country. The Mandate of Heaven inexorably slipped away from them. The beneficiaries were the warlords and one of them, Zhao Kuangyin, was to begin a fifteen year campaign in 960 which reunified the country and led to the foundation of the Sung.

Despite the mistakes the Tang made in their rule from 750 onwards, the work that was accomplished was enormous, as the works of art that have survived amply testify. As has been said Buddhism monopolized both men and materials and since Buddhism was proscribed in 845 large numbers of statues, paintings, monument and frescoes have today disappeared. There remain however, in the way of architecture, several stone buildings of impressive height such as the wooden temples built and rebuilt in Japan (particularly in the region of Kyoto and Nara) on the model of the Chinese originals. In the field of depiction, the frescoes in caves such as those of Dunhuang, which experienced a spectacular development at the time, are still accessible to us. Paintings or copies of paintings have also come down to us, allowing us to distinguish an official style (portraits of emperors, palace scenes in which the Emperor Xuanzong himself appears to have excelled) and landscapes

Less concerned with the dangers of the world, the poets gave free rein to their intimate feelings and the poems are marked by a quite personal delicacy. The following passage is by Li Bo (701-762), who is said to have drowned one evening when he tried to embrace the reflection of the moon in the water whilst drunk:
"Amidst the flowers, a jug of
    wine:
I drink quite alone without a
    friend.
Lifting my cup, I salute the
    moonlight;
My shadow before me: we
    are three . . ."

whose quality reflects the development of this art which was to enjoy its golden age under the Sung.

The subjects of the moment (horses, foreign merchants or tributaries, long-nosed bearded men) are abundantly illustrated in the frescoes and the paintings, although less so than in the ceramic funerary statuettes, which also include numerous exotic animals (camels, lions) and dancers whose full proportions evoke the charms of the concubine Yang Guifei. The three-coloured brown, yellow and green glaze of these figurines is particularly typical of this period.

The Tang empire, which finally collapsed at the beginning of the tenth century left an impression of immense prestige in Asia: the prestige of wise and solid institutions, military glory, economic wealth and the quality of its products. The centuries which were to come left the finest part to the barbarians and their invasions – China was never again to know such influence.

A constant feature of the painted terracotta figurines from the tombs of various members of the imperial family discovered at Qianxian, Sha'anxi, or from the tomb of Zheng Rentai in the district of Liquan, Sha'anxi, is the use of horses being ridden by a variety of figures, such as the archer on the next page, or the lady illustrated above. The figurines of Zheng Rentai display more marked characteristics of the northern tribes.

Northern Horsemen
and the Guard of Honour of the Prince

Opposite: *The muscular horseman carrying a bow displays the features of the member of a northern tribe (height 40 cm.), whilst the riders and horses, both in armour, on this page, have been found in the tomb of Yide prince. Such garments are only found amongst imperial guards of honour.*

On the following pages: *Two horsemen, one with a dog and the other preparing to strike a wild cat. The beard and aquiline nose identify them as members of a northern tribe. They were produced by a special firing technique in which the pigments are mixed directly with the clay, and they are rather unusual examples of Tang ceramics.*

SHA'ANXI

The town of Chang'an in Shenxi was more beautiful than ever when the Sui and then the Tang made it their capital. Splendidly rebuilt at the beginning of the seventh century, it housed palaces, Buddhist monasteries, Taoist sanctuaries and rich residences in great numbers. Archaeological digs were undertaken there at a very early date and they have yielded much evidence of the magnificence of this period. In addition, over the years, new tombs, with their share of artistic treasures, have been discovered.

At this period the heavy traffic along the Silk Route, whose eastern end was Chang'an, meant that foreign influences were very strong. These are particularly apparent in artistic works and in one field at least, the working of gold, they were quite crucial. The working of precious metals was modelled on Sasanian examples from what is now Iran and does not appear to have been developed to a significant degree prior to this time. Although bronze Buddhas had been cast and gilded and jewels were made to house relics, and at times made in large numbers, the number of gold items discovered despite the pillaging of tombs, the quality of their manufacture and the motifs all suggest that the art was then quite new.

On the following pages: *A variety of situations in which the camel is the principal feature. The camel was both ridden and used to carry goods by the great caravans which plied the Silk Route between China and the West. Various statuettes depict these strange animals superbly.*

Opposite: *A laden camel (height 43 cm.).*

Above: *Rider seated on a kneeling camel.*

The craftsmen of the Tang period had plenty of opportunity to familiarize themselves with the various postures and the anatomy of this animal, which was such an important means of transport for trade and cultural contacts, and they were able to depict it most realistically.

230

Horses and Their Ceremonial Harnessings

A neighing horse, a saddled donkey, a horse with an elegantly trimmed and fashioned mane, an elegant saddle cloth of knotted felt and a beautiful set of trimmings worthy of a noble.

The king of the animals portrayed on the walls and in the funerary figurines of the Tang was the horse, the key to the military glory and power of the dynasty. The public studs alone comprised 700,000 of these horses which, to judge from the way they were depicted were large and powerful in their neck, breast and hindquarters. They have somewhat lost the vigour, movement and flying gallop of Han horses, although this may be due to the use of clay instead of bronze, but they have gained in restrained force

and musculature – to the extent that their heads often appear too small. During this period the horse was a genre in its own right just as the first masters of landscape painting, or the religious painters of Buddhist temples; comparable talents were devoted to the horse not just by more or less well-known decorative craftsmen but by scholars who were fully aware of the importance of their extraordinary art.

The figurines of court ladies, the idle hostesses of the tombs of high-ranking persons, enjoyed a particular place of honour in the funerary art of the Tang. This status reflected the important role that they at times played in society and amidst the elite who held power.

Their fate was often unhappy, as was that of the concubine Yang Guifei, who fell with the Emperor Xuanzong; more modestly, the one sung of by Wang Changling (eighth century) regrets having sacrificed love (symbolized by the willows) to her desire for glory:

A variety of pretty female figures (height 42.5-44.5 cm.) decked out in long, coloured garments which touch the ground, as was the fashion at the time. Opposite: One of the 466 statuettes of officials, both civil and military, from the tomb of Zheng Rentai at Liquan, Sha'anxi.

"The young wife in her boudoir
　　does not know distress.
Now, a spring day, in her most beautiful finery,
　　she climbed the floor painted blue.
Suddenly she glimpses near the road,
　　the colour of willows
And she repents of having wanted her husband
　　to leave in search of a title"

The Influence of Persian Gold

These objects, excavated in 1957 south of Xi'an, reveal the influence of Persian gold and silver objects. Both the cup illustrated to the right and the guan vessel opposite use the elephant's head and trunk motif. Both the objects were made using the Tang three-coloured technique.

SPLENDOUR IN THE MIDST OF DANGER

LIAO AND SONG DYNASTIES

"In the area of social life, the arts, diversions, institutions and techniques, China was without any doubt the most advanced country at this time. It was right to think that the rest of the world was populated by Barbarians."

J. Gernet, *Daily life in China on the Eve of the Mongol Invasion*

Between the tenth and thirteenth centuries large areas of northern China were governed by the kingdom of Liao, founded by Qidan, and by the kingdom of Jin, founded by Nuzhen, which fought the Han domination of the Northern and Southern Song dynasties. The funerary practices of the Liao were very varied – brick or stone cells, or urns for ashes in the form of Mongol yurta. This is due to the fact that various different nationalities lived in closely packed communities. The excavations of the tomb of Wei Guo-wang at Chifeng, Liaoning, have unearthed a flask decorated with a cock's comb and eight sets of reins from the early Liao period. These artefacts are nomadic in their inspiration but the porcelain and bronze objects are Tang in style. The Han tombs in the area controlled by the Liao are very similar to those of the central plains and show the cultural and economic links between the two peoples. Thus, tomb 1 in the district of Hure, Jilin has wall paintings of a procession involving more than 60 people of varied appearance and origin, including Qidan servants wearing boots and with their hair gathered around their heads, and Han drummer-boys with sashes and pointed shoes. In the tomb of Yemaotai, in the district of Faku, Liaoning, two silk paintings have been discovered, together with silks and porcelain objects. The tomb itself comprises a front chamber, a rear one and two side ones as well as a principal chamber which contained the coffin. The sides and lids of the marble coffin are covered with coloured reliefs. The lid is in the form of a palace. Broad and deep, it has a pinnacled roof and walls with a door and windows. The occupant was an old lady who was wrapped in dozens of layers of fabric. It is interesting that her cloak opened on the left and is decorated with belts on the back. The boots that she is wearing suggest nomadic dress but there are also Han influences: she is holding pearls, her nostrils are plugged and she is wrapped in a winding sheet. The coffin lid in the form of a palace is also derived from Tang funerary practice.

Silk fabrics were hung on the east and west walls of the main chamber. One is a "blue and green" style landscape which retains the freshness of its original colours. A regional work, it was probably painted by a Kitan hand before the third quarter of the ninth century. The fabrics are of 90 different qualities and the weaving of gold thread and ornamental motifs drawn in gold was not previously known prior to the fourteenth century The porcelain objects fall into four groups: *baiei* (white porcelain), celadon, *liaoci* and *yingqing*. The *baiei* objects from the kilns of Zhongyuan form the bulk of the ceramics intended for everyday use found in the tomb. The *liaoci* ceramics from Zhongyuan. display marked local influence in their forms, decoration and firing. The typical vessel takes the form of a stitched flask, which would date it from the earliest phase of the Liao. The *yingqing* come from Jingdezhen in Jiangxi and the celadon ware from Yaozhou. The porcelain industry made

Detail of one of the numerous wall paintings discovered in the tombs of the Liao dynasty in the course of a season of digging carried out in the winter of 1974 at Zhangjiakou, in the region of Xuanhua, Hebei province.

enormous strides during the period in question and kilns have been found in various regions, from Henan, Sha'anxi, Jiangxi, Guangdong, to Inner Mongolia, each displaying its own, specific style.

In the district of Xuanhua, at Zhangjiakuo, in Hebei a tomb has been discovered with well-preserved wall paintings which cover an area of 86 square metres and on the ceiling of the rear chamber there is a map of the heavens depicting the 28 Xiu (lunar houses), providing evidence for the assimilation of Babylonian astronomy. The map is Chinese in style and is the first stellar map which records observations made both inside China and out. The epitaph reveals that the occupant died in 1116 and his ashes were placed within a carved image — a practice not found in other funerary rites.

The oldest and largest wooden padoga so far discovered in China is the Sakyamuni pagoda in the Fogong temple, in the district of Jingxian, Shanxi. Built in 1065 it was popularly known as the "wooden pagoda of the district of Yingxian". When it was being restored in July 1977 some important relics were discovered inside the statue of Sakyamuni on the fourth floor. These included Buddhist scriptures, paintings and editions.

Recently gold and silver objects and numerous porcelains, as well as Buddhist artefacts, have been found in Song dynasty towers at Dingxian in Hebei, in Wuwei, in Jiangsu and elsewhere. More than 800 relics, including paintings, porcelains, gold and silver objects, have been discovered in the foundations of the Jingzhi and Jingzhongyuan pagodas in the province of Hebei in 1969. The porcelains were produced by the Ding kiln (Yao): one is a green and yellow glazed vase in the form of a parrot 115.6 cm. high. It is very realistic, new in form and vividly coloured. There are a variety of forms of holy water stoups, some with green glazes and incised wave patterns, others wth white glazes and incised decoration. Buddhist artefacts of great importance have been found in a pagoda in the temple of

Bronze figurine of the Buddha Sakyamuni.

Rhuiguang at Suzhou in April 1978. The brick pagoda is modelled on Chinese wooden towers and rises six floors to a height of 43 metres. An inscription on one brick reveals that it was begun in the second year of the reign of Dazhong Xiangfu (1009) and completed in about the eighth year of the reign of Tiansheng (1030). The objects were found in a hiding place on the third floor in which they had been placed before the second floor was built. The hiding place contained two wooden, square boxes, one within the other. The outside of the inner box was decorated in colour with the four *deva* kings, and it contained a group of wooden sculptures, a plinth for Buddhist relics and a two-tiered pedestal 122.6 cm. high overall. Intricately worked, the lower part is in the form of a storm at sea from which immortals stride amid clouds. The upper layer is a mountain on which is an octagonal pavilion intended for a pillar, whose faces bear Buddhist inscriptions. Inside a gourd shaped vase contains nine balls of relics and at the top is a crystal ball with a diameter of 3.4 cm. The hiding place also contained five sutras and a total of 121 volumes. These included the *Saddhamarpundarika* of the Yongxi kingdom of the Northern Song, which is the oldest printed sutra so far known and it does not have the black border found on all other Buddhist sutras.

Wooden figurine of a warrior in the retinue of Buddha.

The Northern Song tombs on the central plains mainly have brick funerary chambers modelled on wooden buildings. The walls are decorated with murals or bricks in relief, which depict scenes from the life of the occupants of the tomb. Relatively few funerary objects have been found in these tombs. One typical example is the tomb of Zhao Da'ong (1099), discovered in 1950 at Baisha, district of Yuxian, Henan. The Sung tombs discovered south of the Changjiang river are principally made of brick with rectangular chambers and vaulted ceilings enclosing large quantities of porcelains, lacquer, gold and silver. In Hunan the majority of the funerary chambers are earth rather than brick. A large quantity of figurines have been discovered in

Sichuan. In 1975, at Fuzhou, Fujian, the tomb of Huang Sheng – a 17 year old girl – was excavated. It contained 418 funerary objects and a large amount of silk, including gauze, fine silk and simple silk with strong, floating and realistic decorations, evidence for the spread of weaving during the Southern Song.

Above: Porcelain cup with a green glaze and incised motifs (height 6.5 cm., diameter 15 cm.). Objects of this type are unusual in southern China and probably came from northern kilns.
Below: Agate cups (height 3-3.6 cm., diameter 4.9-5.4 cm.).

Above: *Pot with a brown glaze modelled in the form of a stitched flask (height 25.5 cm.). The spout is in the form of a cock's head and shows typical Liao culture features.*

Left: Fu *vase in gilded bronze (height 25 cm.) with fine incisions.*

The Liao tombs discovered in 1974 in the region of Xuanhua, Zhangjiakou, Hebei province contained numerous wall paintings which depict the daily life of northern China, near the Great Wall. Processions, receptions, celebrations, groups of musicians, in all of which the tea pot figures constantly.

SONG DYNASTY

960-1276

When one considers the Song dynasty from our twentieth century, one thinks immediately of the celadons and white porcelain or landscape paintings or the "flowers and birds" which contributed to their glory. The Song continued the work of the Tang in the realm of the arts, and, significantly, there were several painters, calligraphers and lovers of art amongst the emperors. The one whose name is best known is the Emperor Huizong, who reigned from 1101 to 1127. As with Xuanzong of the Tang, it was under his reign that the power of the Song collaspsed in northern China. However, on this occasion he was not entirely responsible for the fall of the Song — the causes of which stemmed from the general attitude of the rulers from the beginning of the eleventh century. Although they were able to regain a large part of Chinese territory, the early Song Emperors did not in fact succeed in subjugating their powerful neighbours, the Khitans, who, at the outset, occupied modern Manchuria, north of Hebei and Shanxi. They had founded the Liao dynasty there in 946 and their power was such that the name Khitan was used by several languages at the time to mean China — this was the Cathay of Marco Polo. From 1004 onwards, the Chinese had to pay hundreds of thousands of ounces of silver and rolls of silk in tribute to the Khitan for peace — a tribute that became still heavier with a further tribute to the Xixia, a Tangut people, the masters of Gansu and Chinese Turkestan from 1044.

This yoke, which the Song Emperors did not manage to rid themselves of, was made yet heavier by a serious and what was to be fatal tactical error. They reached agreement with the Jurchen, the ancestors of the last Chinese Empire, behind the backs of the Liao. The Jurchen were powerful and held undisputed sway over the northern part of modern Manchuria. The Liao, caught in a trap, were conquered. Unfortunately, the allies, the Jurchen, turned against the Song and seized the capital, Kaifeng, and the whole of the Yellow River basin in 1127. The whole court was led away as prisoners, including the unfortunate Emperor Huizong. Only one prince, fleeing towards the Yangzi, ended up by establishing himself at Hangzhou, where he founded the southern Song. The tributes to the Jurchen was resumed, heavier than ever, and one might have thought that the new dynasty would sooner or later fall into the lap of the rulers of the North. It rapidly aroused covetousness because of its flourishing trade, well served by the development of paper money, its high quality products (rice, silk, porcelain, manufactured products, paper, tea) and its modernism. But it did not fall and not only did the land of the Song enjoy prosperity but it lasted a century and a half, surviving its old conquerors.

Although weakness of arms cost the Song the partition of the country and an exile in southern China, intellectual life under their aegis had nothing to envy the centuries of the Tang. The renewal of Confucianism weaned minds from the excesses of Buddhist speculation on to the study of the order of things, to the comprehension of the world in a positive and scientific manner. Helped by the development of printing, the commentaries on the Classics, works of synthesis, technical treatises (mathematics, architecture, botany, painting) were offered to an increasingly cultivated and extensive elite. The development of the system of competitions and the prestige attached to official functions encouraged this trend, as did the material comfort of a merchant class that was more important than ever, or even the example of the Song Emperors, who were undoubtedly the most cultivated that history had known. The development of the book also had the effect of launching a romantic and

Portrait of an Empress, wife of Shenzong of the Northern Song, whose reign of nearly twenty years (1068-86) was marked by a virtually unbroken series of disastrous compromises made to stave off the threat of the Khitan and Jurchen tribes of the north.

popular literature, of making the increased numbers of poetic works better known, in particular the sung poems which – and this was a great innovation – appealed to the spoken language. The following poem, composed by Lu You for his son around 1210, expresses the nostalgia felt by many northern Chinese forced to move to the south by the Jurchen:

"After my death, I know, nothing will exist for me;

A scene from a famous masterpiece entitled "Going on the river at the Quing Ming festival", which depicts the liveliness and turmoil of Kaifeng, capital of the Northern Song Empire.

But it pains me not to have seen the reunification of the
    Nine provinces!
The day that the imperial armies, in the north, succeed in
    bringing peace to the Central Plain,
Do not forget to inform your father's protecting divinities!"

If one draws a comparison with the previous Tang dynasty, it appears that the Song gained in refinement what they lost in vigour. Refinement and urbanity in their customs, but also in artistic fields: refinement of expression, of the postures of Buddhist sculpture, the flashing subtlety of the *chan* (*zen*) painting, preciousness without affectation of genre paintings (interiors, women, children, birds, fish, bamboos, flowers and plants). Landscape painters, more numerous than ever, amassed notes and appraisals in their books; many of their paintings are of great distinction and they show a perfect mastery of the brush stroke, whether in

the rough landscapes of the north, or the softer, mist shrouded ones of the lower Yangzi. Finally, one must mention another field, the refined simplicity of ceramics and porcelains, which were greatly appreciated in South-East Asia and Japan, where the finest examples of *tenmoku* and *seiji* would be used for the tea ceremony, that acme of Chinese refinement.

Silk was the Chinese product most frequently used as a means of exchange. In this painting of the Song Emperor Huizong (1101-25) a group of women are pressing a piece of the prized fabric.

251

THE LOWER YANGZI

When the barbarian dynasty of the Jin occupied the north of China they were forced, for better or for worse, to govern disaffected Chinese populations whilst facing the growing threat of the Mongols, the Chinese dynasty of the Song having retreated south of the river Huai in 1127 and established itself in exile. The fleeing Song emperors did not expect to remain in the south for long, which was so different in climate and countryside from the lands that they knew. They even named their capital, which they installed at Hangzhou in the north of Zhejian, Xingzai or "temporary residence." However, they were to stay for almost a century and a half, until the capture of Hangzhou by the Mongol armies in 1276. This period, which saw the long-term establishment of a northern dynasty in the basin of the lower Yangzi, brought considerable benefits to the region, just as had happened previously during the Six Dynasties. The town of Hangzhou, which was so provincial and unimportant in comparison with its prestigious neighbour Nanking, became one of the world's major cities during the thirteenth century, both in terms of population, which is thought to have totalled about a million for the conurbation as a whole, and trade. Its communications with the hinterland were ensured by a dense network of canals and by the Yangzi, whilst at the same time it developed its long-standing sea links with Arab and Persian merchants.

A variety of Buddhist relics were discovered by chance in a hiding place on the third floor of the temple of Rui-guang at Suzhou. Amongst these were (from left to right) the painted and gilded clay statuette of the Goddess of Mercy, a bronze figurine of Sakyamuni, wooden figurines of the King Deva (here holding a pagoda in his hand), and a bronze figurine of Ksitigarbha holding a pearl in her hand.

The relics found at Suzhou were contained in two boxes, one within the other. The inner one (above) (height 124 cm.) is decorated on four sides with figures of the King Deva drawn with sinuous lines in the style of Wu Daozi, a famous Tang master. Inside the pillar there were inscribed Buddhist sutras (right, detail of the tip crowned by a crystal ball).

Despite the slackening of the great fervour
for Buddhism of earlier centuries, it remained one of
the major religions of the period or rather one should say,
one of the major components of the religious syncretism,
and there were hundreds of Buddhist foundations in
Hangzhou and its environs. The iconographic style had
evolved since the Tang and it showed, just as many other
aspects of culture did, the influence of southern China;
becoming more complicated in order to satisfy the taste of
the lower classes, where Buddhism remained deeply rooted.

*The octagonal pedestal of the pillar
depicts a sea in the middle of which a
hill rises supported by eight lions.
Above: A case for Buddhist sutras
in lacquer with mother-of-pearl en-
crustations (length 35 cm.).*

*Opposite: Wood carving of a warrior
escorting the Buddha, with a massive
body and covered with long, wavy ribbons.*

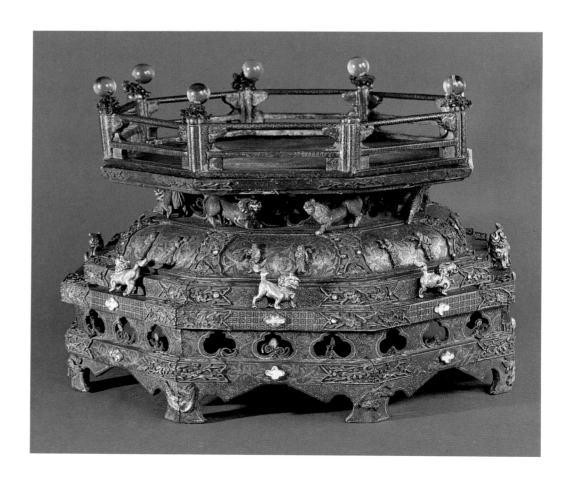

YUAN DYNASTY

1276-1368

Genghis Khan (1167-1227) managed to unite the power of the Mongols and extended his empire from Samarkand to Korea, including the whole of China to the north of the Yellow River. Opposite: Genghis Khan seated on the imperial throne together with his consort.

Kublai Khan, who extended his conquests into southern China, completing the process in around 1278.

Who could have withstood the Mongols? The hordes of Genghis Khan left death and desolation in their wake. However, with its hundred million or so inhabitants, its mountains and valleys, its numerous water courses to be crossed, and the spirit of resistance to the invader which the Chinese had acquired over the centuries, China was a large mouthful for even the Mongols to swallow. 43 years passed between the taking of Kaifeng, the capital of the Jurchen empire, in 1233, and the fall of Hanghzou, capital of the Southern Song, in 1276.

Many Chinese could have died in the invasion since the Mongols did not shrink from mass execution. However, the new conquerors rapidly understood what profit they could derive from this rich conquest. Clumsy at first in this land of settled peoples, they surrounded themselves with Muslim or Khitan intermediaries, placed Mongol officials in the administration, and undertook to Mongolize Chinese institutions: more rigid administration, a more severe penal code and, above all, taxation that became crushing for Southern

China. To help extract the taxes in kind which they levied, they embarked on the digging of a new Grand Canal in 1279. The Mongols felt themselves so at home in this rich country that they decided to establish their capital in China in 1264. This was Yanjing, modern Peking, the old capital of the Jurchen, renamed "Town of the Khan", Khanbalik in Mongol and Dadu or "Great Metropolis" in Chinese. They also took the dynastic name of Yuan. Restored from 1267 onwards, the capital contained the splendid palace of the Khan of which Marco Polo gave this amazed description in his *Travels*:

"Know that it is the largest that ever was. . . the roof is very high. The walls of the palace and the rooms are all covered with gold and silver. . . The hall is so large that six thousand people could dine there with comfort. There are so many rooms that it is marvellous to behold. . ."

So many rich merchants and landed proprietors escaped tax or were able to profit from the situation that the peasantry were placed under enormous pressure, made yet worse by the confiscation of lands. Gradually, the peasants sought the protection of numerous sects and secret societies, one of which, the Red Turbans, sparked the general rebellion of 1350.

Compared with the brilliant period of the Song which had preceded them, the era of the Yuan resembles a cultural desert. Only in the fields of popular literature and the theatre were new works added in large numbers. The masters of Confucian thought were forgotten and the studies of the Classics virtually abandoned. Landscape painters took to the mountains or rivers in seclusion and painted mainly for themselves. However, the unbroken encouragement of technical studies allowed the scientific work which had been begun under the Song to continue, particularly in the fields of mathematics and astronomy. This effort was unfortunately halted under the Ming and therefore did not benefit China as much as it ought to have. However, although this was the only claim to glory of the

Mongol invaders, the growth of Chinese technology made a considerable contribution to medieval Europe in conjunction with the development in relations between China and the Muslim and Christian West. It permitted the transmission to the West of crucial discoveries, beginning with the compass and the rudder in the twelfth century followed by gunpowder, sluice gates, improved iron casting, printing

with movable type; paper, made in China since the second century, was passed on by the Muslim world to be imported and then made in Europe at the end of the thirteenth. By their writings, the Western travellers to "Cathay" recorded this technological lead for posterity. Marco Polo, of course, was one such, but there was also Ibn Battuta, the Franciscans Odoric de Pordenone, Jean de Moncorvin and many more.

Marco Polo visited the great Kublai Khan in his capital of Khanbalik (present day Beijing) and, as an acute observer, he was able to describe the life of the nomads of Central Asia, the palace of the Great Khan, the ceremonies and the court festivals, as well as the customs and resources of China and the countries through which he journeyed. This French miniature, which illustrates the story of the Venetian traveller, shows a mulberry bark coin bearing the imperial seal.

In the Yuan tomb excavated at Jiaozhuo, Henan, the bricks of the funerary
chamber give a lively impression of the
celebrations and entertainments of the
Mongol nobility: on this page there are
a variety of musicians and actors.

More actors, domestics and dancers in various postures. The servants, in the centre, are identified by the bottles they are holding in their hands. The highly realistic depiction allows the individual instruments to be made out.

MING GLORY

THE LAST CHINESE DYNASTY

At the foot of Mt. Tianshoushan, about 50 km. north west of Beijing, there are 13 imperial tombs of the Ming dynasty (1368-1644). The tomb of the first emperor, Zhu Yuanzhang, is at Nanjing and bears the name of Xialing. The site was chosen by the Emperor Cheng Zu for his tomb after he had transferred the Ming capital from Nanjing to Beijing. From then on thirteen successive emperors of the Ming dynasty were buried there. Work on excavating the underground palace was begun in May 1956 and it was formally opened to the public as a museum in 1959. Dingling is the tomb of the Emperor Wan Li, who ascended the throne at the age of 12 and ruled for 48 years (1537-1620). Building began when he was only 22 and was completed in the space of six years. The building which stood above it, the Lingen Hall, burned down in 1914, leaving behind just the remains of its foundations, which are still visible. The principal visible trace of a tomb is the Minglon. This contains a stone stela and its two sides are linked to the Baocheng — a wall which runs around the pine and cypress covered tumulus with a circumference of 75 metres. It is beneath this tumulus that the undergound palace lies. Excavations of the tomb began from the inner part of the Baocheng, at the point where a stone tunnel was discovered with the inscription "Between this tablet and the wall of Jinggang there are 16 zhang (about 52.8 metres) and 3.5 zhang (about 11.95 metres) in depth." A sloping tunnel, again in stone, was also uncovered at a depth of twenty metres. The two tunnels formed the passageway through which the coffins were lowered into the underground palace.

The front and central halls are linked so as to form a rectangular corridor at the end of which the rear hall runs cross-wise. The three halls are connected by three marble portals, on whose inner sides there was a stone bar 160 cm. long whose lower end is set in the filling material. When the door was closed the bar slid into its seat, locking the door so that it could not be opened from the outside.

On the platform of the rear hall there are the coffins of the Emperor Zhu Yijuan and the two empresses and around them are displayed gold and silver objects, porcelains, jewelled pendants, brocades. About 300 objects have been excavated. For the most part they are basins, cups, spoons and *jue* vessels made of gold or silver, all elaborately embossed and some even set with rubies and sapphires. A gold crown of the emperor and four crowns in very fine filigree for the empresses, are the most conspicuous objects.

Tombs of the Ming princes have been found in various places. A highly important one is the tomb of Prince Zhu Yuellan, the eldest son of the Prince of Shu, which was discovered at Chengdu in Sichuan. The fact that this palace tomb was intended for a 22 year old prince gives one an idea of the burial system of princes at the beginning of the dynasty. It contained numerous funerary objects, including 400 porcelain figurines of various types. The excavation of the tomb of Zhu Tan, Prince of Lu, in Shandong has yielded 430 painted figurines and precious, painted books and calligrams including hollyhocks and butterflies painted on a fan together with a poem in the handwriting of the Song Emperor Zhao Gou and a book entitled *Poetry of Du Fu, Annotations of a Thousand Men* and further *Annotations of Huang* printed during the Yuan dynasty.

From the tomb of Zhu Houye, Prince of Yi, in the city of Nancheng, Yianxi, more than 250 gold or silver objects have been excavated. Recently, the tombs of Zhu Yiyin, King Yixuan and that of Zhu Youmu, King Yiding have been discovered and they have provided information on the tombs of the Ming vassal states.

Statues of warriors and a variety of animals guard certain imperial Ming tombs. Although the quality is poorer than in earlier periods, they are still spectacular and testify to the power of the deceased sovereign.

BEIJING

Peking ("Capital of the North") had as many names as masters and, its position near the border making it an easy target for the barbarians, many of its masters have followed one another, possibly after razing the old city in order to build a new one. Known as Ji during the Warring States period, it was destroyed by the First Emperor, Qin Shi Huangdi. It was then rebuilt in 70 BC and called Yan, then Youzhou after the Han. The Khitan destroyed it in 986 and then rebuilt it, naming it, by a strange quirk of history, Nanjing, since it was the "Capital of the South" of their kingdom. It then became Yanjing. Enlarged by the Jurchen in twelfth century, it was known as Zhongdu, "Capital of the Centre" (i.e. the centre of the Jurchen empire) or rather Daxingfu. Genghis Khan gobbled it up in 1215 but his grandson restored its dignity and founded Khanbalik, Dadu in Chinese, the capital of the Yuan Mongol empire. Then it became a secondary town until 1421, when a Ming emperor made it the Capital of the North, Beijing. The modern city, with some ten million inhabitants is very aware of its role as capital. It is a serious and solemn town, an indispensible quality for a capital in the eyes of the Chinese.

MING DYNASTY

1368 - 1644

Zhu Yuanzhang, the Emperor Taizu, was the founder of the Ming dynasty. Opposite: The building of palaces was the favourite pastime of several Ming emperors. This one, which appears suspended amidst the clouds, is in the same style as the imperial palace of the Forbidden City built by Cheng-zu.

Zhu Yuanzhang, a peasant from Anhui, won the race for the imperial throne in 1368. It should be said that the situation was ideal for a daring chieftain since the failure of the nomadic Yuan to administer China was obvious. Although it took him twenty years to reach the throne this was mainly because several other chieftains had the same idea as he did. However, once everything had settled down, he chose the name Ming for his dynasty. The offensives which brought the empire new territories in Manchuria and northern Vietnam were followed by a period of defence. The Mongols grew more aggressive again and one of their incursions in 1449 even ended in the capture of the Emperor Yingzong, who remained their prisoner until 1457. Walls had to be rebuilt against them in Hebei, Shanxi and Shenxi. This was the decline.

With the sixteenth century more serious troubles began for the Ming Emperors. First of all, inside the country, the economy underwent great changes which the authorities were unable either to foresee or to control. The authoritarian centralism of the government weakened, and taxes slipped away, lost between the local powers and counter powers, in contraband and clandestine activity. Furthermore, the costs of the counterattacks against the Japanese armies of Toyotomi Hideyoshi in Korea, of the fight against piracy, of meeting local uprisings and of the fabulous projects (palaces, tombs) pursued by the emperors finally ruined the public finances. Neither the efforts of some emperors or the energetic action of certain good ministers could reverse this trend. The Ming empire declined, while in the north-east the Jurchen, the masters of Manchuria, were recovering their strength at the expense of the Mongols. In 1644 they seized Peking and power.

Ming Treasures

Opposite: Hu vase with incised dragon and cloud patterns, studded with pearls, jade and red and blue gems, and a gold hairpin.

The grave goods of the various tombs of the members of the imperial family comprise an immense array of objects, including a gold fu vase (above) and a blue and white ceramic one with floral motifs (right). Top: A ceramic gu vessel (height 25.2 cm.) with a yellow glaze and decorated with figures on horseback, flowers and plants drawn in violet.

274

Imperial crowns

Below: *Crown of gold links.*
Opposite: *One of the four phoenix crowns, decorated with three gold dragons and two pearl phoenixes. Each crown has more than 5,000 pearls and a hundred precious stones.*

Acknowledgements

All the photographs reproduced in this book were supplied by Cultural Relics
Publishing House, Beijing, except the following:

Pages 58, 95, 189, 263: Bibliothèque Nationale, Paris

Page 273: British Museum, London

Page 161: Chavannes, E., *Les documents chinois découverts par Aurel Stein dans les
sables du Turkestan oriental*, Oxford 1913

Page 108: (2nd and 3rd from left): Walter Dräyer, Zurich

Page 90: Geil, W.E., *The Great Wall of China*, London 1909

Page 251: Museum of Fine Arts, Boston

Page 188: National Palace Museum, Taipei

Page 94: *San Cai Tu Hui* (catalogue), vol. II

Page 107: Else Tholstrup, Copenhagen

Page 218: Tokyo National Museum, Tokyo

Pages 16-17, 93: Yugoslav Review, Belgrade

The publishers would also like to thank
Du Pont de Nemours Italiana, Milan
for their invaluable technical assistance.